P9-DCY-732

change your home! enhance your life! with tools, tips, and inspiration from Barbara K!

barbara

k ™

room for improvement ™

Notice

The writers and editors who compiled this book have tried to make all the contents as accurate and correct as possible. Photographs and text have been carefully checked and cross-checked. However, due to the variability of personal skill, tools, materials, and so on, neither the writers nor Rodale Inc. assume any responsibility for any injuries suffered or for damages or other losses that result from the material presented herein. All instructions should be carefully studied and clearly understood before beginning any project. Mention of specific companies, organizations, or authorities in this book does not imply endorsement by the publisher, nor does mention of specific companies, organizations, or authorities imply that they endorse this book. Internet addresses and telephone numbers given in this book were accurate at the time it went to press.

© 2005 by Barbara Kavovit
Photographs © 2005 by Rodale Inc.

All rights reserved. No part of this publication may be reproduced or transmitted in any form or by any means, electronic or mechanical, including photocopying, recording, or any other information storage and retrieval system, without the written permission of the publisher.

Printed in the United States of America
Rodale Inc. makes every effort to use acid-free ♾, recycled paper ♻.

Book design by Ellen Nygaard

Illustrations by Nick Higgins
Interior photographs by Lewis Bloom and George Ross
Cover photograph by Arthur Elgort; makeup by Sonia Kashuk; hair by Maria Barca

Library of Congress Cataloging-in-Publication Data

Barbara K
    Room for improvement : change your home! enhance your life! with tools, tips, and inspiration from barbara k! / Barbara K
        p.   cm.
    Includes index.
    ISBN-13 978–1–59486–133–8 paperback
    ISBN-10 1–59486–133–1 paperback
    1. Dwellings—Maintenance and repair—Amateurs' manuals.   2. Do-it-yourself work.
3. Women.   I. Title.
    TH4817.3B36   2005
    643'.7—dc22
    2004030631

Distributed to the book trade by Holtzbrinck Publishers

2 4 6 8 10 9 7 5 3 1   paperback

We inspire and enable people to improve their lives and the world around them

For more of our products visit **rodalestore.com** or call 800-848-4735

To my dad. Thank you, Dad, for all your support, love, and patience throughout the years, and for all the building projects and blocks you gave me. I love you more than words can say.

To my mom for encouraging me to keep swimming on all those cold days and for her support, love, and patience. Mom, you were my first role model for an independent woman and I love you!

And to Zachary Kavovit-Murphy—my beautiful son and newest inspiration. You are the absolute love and light of my life.

Contents

Acknowledgments

First, I would like to thank my mom and dad for giving me love and support throughout my life. Thank you also to my awesome sister, Caryn, for always being there for me over the years.

Special thanks to Sam Gradess—you were not only one of my very first investors but also someone who encouraged me with your wise counsel, which enabled me to have greater clarity over the years. Your endless and tireless support, total understanding, and commitment to the barbara k! brand and to me helped get me through periods of uncertainty. Thank you so very much for your personal encouragement when it mattered the most; you are a true friend.

I would also like to thank the following people for their endless hours and effort in making this book possible:

Mel Berger, my literary agent at the William Morris Agency: Mel, thank you for believing in the brand, this book, and me.

Margot Schupf, my editor at Rodale: Wow! Now I know you are the best editor in the world. Thanks for all your focus, awesome commitment, believing in me, and seeing this project through.

Ellen Nygaard, book designer, thanks for all your creativity. To everyone else at Rodale: Thank you for all your hard work, creativity, and dedication.

Karen Kelly: A special thanks to you for doing such a great job capturing my voice and organizing my thoughts on paper. You brought things out of me that I don't think anyone else could have.

Lewis Bloom and George Ross, the photographers: You both made me look and feel great.

Michelle Bergerson at Cityscape Design: Thank you for your beautiful designs, commitment, and energy in making this book a success.

barbara k! Thanks

Rome was not built in a day and neither was barbara k! It takes a small army and many dedicated people to build a brand. I have been very fortunate to attract "entrepreneurs" in their own right who have assisted me in reaching my goals. They are a group of optimistic people who focus on solutions, not problems. Everyone at barbara k! over the past two years has been loyal, patient, and dedicated. These are wonderful people whom I respect and admire and who have appreciated my vision to go the distance and be team players. To them I owe enormous thanks.

Additional Thanks

There are a few people in my professional life that I have to single out and thank as they have been with me throughout most of my entrepreneurial years stemming from my construction days.

BJ Toner: You have been with me since *very* early on in my business life and youth. Thanks for being a person I can rely on and trust and for keeping me organized in some of my more insane moments! Your loyalty will always be appreciated, and thanks for sticking by me through all the good times and not so good times!

Takeesha Banks: "My Keesha Girl." You are a shining star! You have been there every hour, every minute, every day. You are so much more than my assistant but a stable support for me. You are my "sister" and friend. Simply put, I could not have had my personal and professional life so completely organized. Thanks for your endless love and support of me. You are a true role model for the independent woman!

Kurt Straub: You have been working with me since the construction days and I am thrilled we are still together! Thanks for all your endless days on the photo shoots making sure all the projects came off without a hitch. Your loyalty and commitment are so appreciated throughout so many years in the construction days.

Kevin Glaser: Seems like only yesterday when we first met on the slopes and suddenly I had a company with more than one person. Thanks for all your past commitment and dedication to the brand and to me. I will never forget our first trip to Taiwan, all the fun we've had, and where we came from. You will always be considered an integral part of barbara k!

Still More Thanks

Brad Rose: It's not often that you meet an attorney who becomes instrumental in helping you reach your goals and has the same sense of urgency you do. Thank you for all your guidance and thanks to Pryor Cashman Sherman Flynn for believing in me and going the distance.

TestRite International: Special thanks to Judy Lee and the entire TestRite staff for their belief in me at such an early stage. Thanks for your patience and guidance and for making superior quality products.

John Lonczak: Thank you for your knowledge and expertise in product design.

Thanks to all the retailers who took a chance on an unknown named Barbara K, particularly Charlie Chinni and JCPenney, for giving us our first chance at retail.

Bill and Sheila McCaffery from McCaffery Ratner Gottlieb & Lane: Thanks for nurturing me through my first advertising campaign.

To my investors: Thank you very much for believing in me and supporting me throughout the growth of barbara k!

Zeny and Fernando: Thanks for keeping me on time and organized.

Maria Barca: Thanks for always making sure I shine!

Finally, special thanks to my loyal customers who have helped me make my dreams a reality.

My Story

Here I am about to inspire you to take control of the home around you and make your dream house a reality. A lot of people who knew me "when" may think I am the most unlikely person to do that, based on my academic track record. My high school teachers would say to my mom, "She's a smart girl . . . but she can't seem to focus." Of course I couldn't—I was already dreaming up my first business!

I am the founder of a brand and lifestyle company for women called barbara k! But I'm also the girl next door listening to rock and roll at a party, whom you said hello to on the beach or spotted shopping at the mall. I'm a happy-go-lucky kid from the Bronx who had no more opportunity than anybody else, but who turned an idea into a Big Business. Do you recognize yourself in my description? Most likely, you do.

Some people say I've been lucky. If being lucky means recognizing and then seizing an opportunity, then, yes, I'm the luckiest person in the world. The first ingredient to fulfilling your personal dreams and becoming a successful entrepreneur is being aware of the possibilities around you every day. The second is acknowledging and appreciating what you're good at and turning it into the basis of something great. For me, it was a childhood skill with Legos.

Accomplishment and self-esteem go hand in hand. That's where *Room for Improvement* comes in. This book will show you how easy it is to use tools around the house, which will enable you to improve your environment. And that will help give you the independence you need to take charge of your life. Facing big issues such as job loss, divorce, financial problems, or just day-to-day challenges will be easier once you have gained the confidence and self-reliance that comes from self-sufficiency. I know it's true—I've seen it happen in my own life and in other women's lives.

This conviction comes from every experience I've had. I was a dreamer as a child—a cockeyed optimist, in fact. I still am. I was raised in the Bronx, which taught me some hard-core life lessons. If you wanted something—anything—there was probably going to be a fight for it. Ensuring the neighborhood bullies didn't push me off my bike was part of everyday life. That and the fact that there was so much emphasis placed on academics by my mother, a history teacher and later an assistant principal of a tough school in the Bronx, helped mold my character.

My dad also had a hand in my future. He was good at building things, and he always included me in his projects. Once he built my sister, Caryn, and me a bunk bed. He would point to a part of it and say, "Barbara, Caryn—nail this." We would take turns with his hammer and bang away. The awkward feeling of the outsized, heavy hammer in my hand was dwarfed in comparison to the great sense of accomplishment I felt when I was finished. It's a feeling I remember and cherish to this day.

Learning to swim also taught me to push for my dreams, even when faced with hardship. My mother would take Caryn and me to Red Cross–sponsored swimming lessons in Montauk, New York. The lessons were held early in the summer season, but no matter how cold or rainy it was, my mom would be out there with us making sure we went through our strokes. This taught me persistence and physical and emotional strength. Nothing is easy, and that goes for swimming in a chilly ocean, but you have to keep going if you want to achieve anything. So today, when things get a little challenging at work, I tell my staff to "keep swimming."

After college, I tried my hand on Wall Street, but it wasn't for me. At the same time, in 1989, there was a construction boom in New York. My mother and her friends complained about contractors and repairmen who didn't show up. A light-bulb went off over my head. I thought, "I can do something about this. What about a *woman* helping *women* get projects done around the house?"

I had the local copy shop make up flyers and business cards. I named the business Stand-Ins. I put my brochures in every mailbox within a 10-mile radius of my house, and I'd stand in the parking lots of upscale shopping centers in my area and introduce myself to every woman and give her my card. I would say, "I'm Barbara and I can help you fix anything in your house." No job was too small or too big: I'd clean and fix anything, repair cracked tiles, clean gutters, and change doorknobs.

My instincts were right: I got a *lot* of calls. Suddenly, I had jobs but no real home repair experience. So I got a copy of the local *Penny Saver* and called every handyman listed. I told them I would find and take them to jobs (often because I wanted to make sure they showed up) and bring them home again. I supervised their work and made sure every job got done. I learned home repair, communication skills, and plain old-fashioned market research simply by diving in and learning by doing. I was eager to put on a tool belt with a hammer and tape measure hanging from it. I thought it was a really cool and sexy look.

After the business took off, I wrote a letter to the head buyer for the IBM headquarters located near my home. I told him Stand-Ins could assist in any repairs at a moment's notice. I followed up with a phone call but had no luck. Did it stop me? No. After an unrelenting campaign of calls and letters, I wore him down and was invited in for a meeting. He asked me point blank, "What can you do for IBM?" I said, "I can repair and improve your offices on a moment's notice. Anything you need fixed, I can fix." The result was a 2-year small repair contract at the IBM corporate headquarters.

Things started happening very quickly after that. For example, a business associate told me about a developer in Weehawken, New Jersey, who was looking for women contractors. There were advantages to hiring women and minorities, especially when the developer had union problems (like this one did). I didn't know what a union was, but when I met with the developer, he told me I would have to negotiate with its leaders. I gave it my best shot and was awarded a $3 million contract. By 1993 I had been in business for 2 years. I bought a van, leased an office, and hired a couple of carpenters and project managers. It was difficult since I was in a tough, male-dominated industry. And I got bruises—men called me names and threatened me. Just like growing up in the Bronx. I took it in stride. When you're on to something, it's to be expected.

Eventually I decided to take a chance on New York City real estate. I formed a new company, Anchor Construction, which focused on corporate and commercial construction. I was finally breaking through the "glass ceiling." Anchor landed construction projects for high-profile corporations such as HotJobs, iVillage, Bloomingdales, Carnegie Hall, and others. These companies liked the fact that Anchor was woman-owned and -operated. They counted on me to always do my best on a job . . . even though there may have been problems during the course of the job.

During this time, I met my former husband, who was an inspiration to me in the rough-and-tumble construction world. And we had our son, Zachary. By 2000 I was doing millions of dollars' worth of business and earned a name in the industry. *Crain's Business* even cited me as being one of the "100 Most Influential Women in Business in New York City."

Despite these successes, I kept thinking about the women from my early days. Why did they have to rely on no-show contractors, husbands, brothers, fathers, or neighbors? Generations of women have been fearful of anything going wrong in their home—yet few of them have the knowledge or skills to do anything about it. Feeling comfortable about doing home improvement was the "final frontier" for women. I saw an opportunity to "change the gene pool" and recreate the way women felt about using tools. That meant convincing women that tools could change their life and that they were just accessories like their shoes, belts, bags, and emery boards. They simply could not survive without them!

I knew women would respond to great-looking products that also worked and were made just for them. A hammer is so big and ugly—why can't it look and feel good in your hand? Why couldn't I recreate what women have come to expect to see from tools without changing their function? Wouldn't tools like that appeal to women's practical *and* creative sides? It's important for women to realize the many applications for tools. For example, how good would it feel to say, "Yes, I can help you with that" when your children ask you to raise a bicycle seat or fix a toy?

Then, almost simultaneously, 9/11 happened and the construction business, my marriage, as well as life itself seemed to collapse. One evening during that difficult time, I was watching *Sex and the City*. The character Samantha was trying unsuccessfully to hang a curtain; she had to call her boyfriend who would not come over and help her. I thought, "This is a totally modern, independent woman, and she can't put up a curtain rod!" And it all clicked into place. I knew I was right. If she had the perfect, stylish tool kit, she could do it herself.

That idea prompted me to call a prototype maker. He asked me if I had an engineered drawing of the tool kit case that I had in mind. I didn't, so I went on a quest and found someone to make a CAD drawing. Finally, my idea was translated into one beautiful $8,000 kidney-shaped tool case. A "star" (my tool case) was born.

After intense research, I located a manufacturer and a sourcing company called TestRite in Taipei, Taiwan. In no time, I was sitting in their boardroom. The president of the company was a woman, and even though we came from two very different cultures, she immediately understood what I was trying to accomplish. She took one look at the tool kit and said, "This is the best idea I have ever seen." Right then and there, she committed to making the molds for a set of tools based on the original tool case design. TestRite was instrumental in getting the product side of my business off the ground.

Ultimately barbara k! and *Room for Improvement* are about self-determination and independence. Tools are simply one way of helping you get there. It's not about perfection. It's not about being "tool girl" and walking around with a skill saw. It's about stepping-stones. It's about making mistakes, learning from them, and getting it right the next time. "Fix my running toilet"—done! "Hang my picture"—done! "Tell him 'I have had enough'"—done! "Get that new job"—done!

Life changes like the ocean—so fast! It takes a great set of tools to get you through it. Becoming a self-sufficient, independent woman is probably the greatest gift I gave myself. I hope that *Room for Improvement* inspires you to fearlessly enhance your home and go after your dreams so that you too can take charge of your life.

Keep on swimming!

Barbara K

Chapter 1
Tools Rule

Every tool is a "power tool" in my opinion. That's because, when used properly, the right tool can help you fix a broken doorknob, un-squeak a squeaky door, or help hang meaningful photographs and mementos on the walls of your home. The result? You'll start your day off on the right foot because you won't be battling a flimsy doorknob or a faulty lock, you'll no longer be annoyed by the noisy door, and you'll be surrounded by beautiful things that you love. And it all starts when you pick up a hammer!

I truly believe that tools can change your life. Sure, you can call a handyman (and most likely it *will* be a man), and he can replace some rotting molding around your door. You can hire a plumber to rid your sink of a nasty clog or replace some ancient bathroom fixtures. You can pay some teenagers to paint your living room. You can wait *forever* for someone else in your household (names will not be mentioned!) to get off the couch and fix it (whatever *it* is) for you. Or *you can make your dream home a reality yourself!*

Why wait? Knowing how to do your own simple home repairs and decorating and design jobs gives you control over your own life and home. Wouldn't it be liberating *not* to have to depend on the skills and the empty promises of a stranger when it comes to your home? And even if you choose to hire people to perform certain repair jobs, wouldn't it be great to know whether or not they are doing the jobs properly and you're getting your money's worth?

So let's start at the beginning, with the tools of your new trade.

How to Select Tools

Having the right tools will help you perform both simple tasks and more complex jobs with ease and security. Shoddy tools or those that are wrong for a particular job may break; worse, they can cause you to hurt yourself if you're not able to use them properly. But high-quality tools, carefully chosen and appropriate for both you and the job at hand, will make your life easier while adding enjoyment to your design and decorating jobs. The right tools, used according to the manufacturers' instructions, are paramount to your safety, performance, and success.

So how do you select the right tools? Once you've decided what you need (we'll talk about which tools in detail in "Barbara K's Basic Tool Kit" on page 22), go to the store and *handle* the tools. Are all the edges smooth? Do the tools feel good in your hand? Do the power tools come with warranties? There is no reason why a set of tools shouldn't last a long time and be passed on to the next generation. Wouldn't you love to know that your daughter or son will someday use the same tools you so proudly put to work in making their childhood home a wonderful place to live?

ARE YOU A BAG OR BOX WOMAN?

Once you have your tools assembled, you should keep them somewhere close at hand so that you can grab them quickly when a doorknob comes loose or a hole needs patching. Should you invest in a snappy metal or heavy-duty plastic toolbox or should you choose a snazzy and soft canvas or leather tool bag? Either way, you should be proud to show off your tools and their carrying case. Personally, I prefer to keep my tools in my hard, slim blue plastic case that slips easily into a kitchen drawer and looks great when I pull it out (or displayed on the countertop). But there are pros and cons to both options.

Some women feel that a toolbox, with its rigid sides and layers of storage, is excellent for keeping smaller bits and pieces organized. But other women I know say that metal boxes can rust, and metal toolboxes can scratch floors when moved around. One way to alleviate this problem is by sticking soft circular pads to the bottom of the box. (These adhesive circular pads are often used on the bottom of chair legs and other furniture to prevent floors from being scratched.)

A sturdy canvas or leather bag won't mar your floor or rust. But unless it has lots of pockets for smaller tools, such as a nail set or a compass and tiny bits like nails and screws, these items may fall to the bottom of the bag and become nearly impossible to find. But if you do choose the bag option, you will have a lot of choices. Canvas bags come in all shapes and sizes, and you don't necessarily have to buy one in a hardware store. You can express your style by using a colorful beach bag or a canvas tote found at your favorite boutique.

Finally, if you're going to store your tools outside in a garage or shed, a metal or plastic box will be less susceptible to weather changes. If you plan on keeping your tools inside your house in a hall closet or even a drawer, a bag could be a better option for you.

Setting Up a Workspace

No matter where you put your workspace, take the time to personalize the area and make it your own. There's no law that says a work area has to be grim and gray. In fact, it should be a happy, fun area—one you look forward to using! Consider painting work surfaces in your favorite color. A brown worktable is boring; a lavender one isn't! If your workspace does double duty in the kitchen or family room, don't despair. You can find tarps (for protecting surfaces) in many colors. And canvas drop cloths can be painted or dyed to suit your fancy. If you take the time to personalize your space and make it attractive, you'll be more prone to use it.

Here are some practical considerations in setting up a workspace of your own.

- Make sure your space is well lit. Being able to see what you are doing is of paramount importance for the sake of both safety and accuracy.
- If you are working at a table that is used for something else (such as food preparation or after-school homework), make sure you have a drop cloth or tarp to place over the table when working. This protects the surface, of course, and also makes cleanup easier: You can simply gather up your tarp and slide any waste into the trash.
- Put a Shop-Vac on the top of your to-buy list; they're relatively inexpensive and will make wet or dry cleanup a snap. And you won't have to worry about destroying that expensive vacuum that you use around your home.
- Have a wide-mouthed trash receptacle nearby. Cleanup will be easy, especially if you line it with contractor's grade bags. They are tough and virtually impossible to tear. The good news is you can find them in any home improvement store.
- An easily accessible power strip is a must. The cords on power tools are usually quite short. So sturdy 6- to 10-foot extension cords will allow you to move around easily and safely with your power drill or sander.
- If your workspace is in a garage or shed, some kind of heat source, such as a space heater, will come in handy when the autumn winds begin to blow and temperatures are cooler.

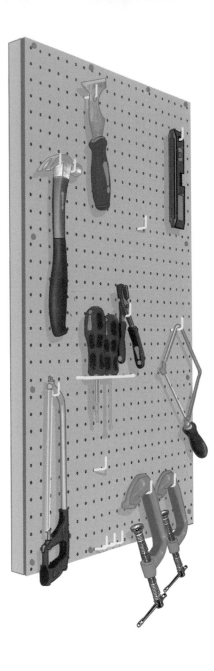

We've Got You Pegged!
Make a Peg-Board Tool Storage Rack
Time: About 3 hours

Setting up a tool and material storage area on the back of a closet door, in a spare bedroom, or even in your basement is a simple, inexpensive process. Peg-Board is a great material that can be cut to any size and painted any color under the sun. Its small holes hold a variety of metal hooks and holders especially designed to hold tools and other objects securely.

Peg-Board racks can hold more than tools: Craft supplies, beauty supplies, children's toys, and kitchen equipment can find a home on this simple hanging system.

What You Need
Tape measure
Peg-Board, cut to desired size
1- by 2-inch furring strips
Stud finder
12 2-inch screws (masonry or regular, depending on surface)
Anchors (if not screwing Peg-Board into studs or masonry)
Power drill with screwdriver bits or 6-in-1 screwdriver
Safety glasses
Miter box and saw
12 ¾-inch wood screws for Peg-Board
Assorted Peg-Board hooks and holders, depending on your needs

How to Get It Done
1. To make the rack, first measure the wall where you will install your rack with a tape measure. Position the rack according to your height. You shouldn't have to reach uncomfortably to get at the top-most items on the board.
2. Once you have determined the height and width of the space available, take your measurement to the hardware store and have them cut the Peg-Board to size. You may have to buy an entire sheet, which often comes in 4- by 8-foot pieces. The remaining pieces can be used for another board somewhere else in the house—in the kitchen, office, or inside a closet door. While you are at the hardware store, pick

up a length of 1- by 2-inch furring strip, enough to frame the inside perimeter of the cut Peg-Board

3. If you are screwing the frame into drywall, find the wooden studs in the wall with a stud finder. Studs are typically located every 16 inches from the center of the wall (depending on the building code in your town). Screwing into studs is the most secure way to hang a rack that will hold heavy tools. If the place where you have chosen to install your rack does not match up with the wall studs, you will also have to use anchors to hold the screws in place.

   If you are screwing the frame into masonry, such as a concrete garage or basement wall, you will need to use masonry drill bits. (See "Screwing into Drywall and Masonry" on page 6 for specific how-to on screws and anchors.)

4. Put on safety glasses. Cut the furring strips to fit around the outside edge of the Peg-Board with a miter box and saw. Create a frame and screw it into the wall where the Peg-Board will go. Use 2-inch screws made for screwing into wall studs or masonry screws if you're screwing it into masonry. Screw all four corners of the frame into place and then screw it in two equidistant places on all four sides. There is no need to attach the pieces to each other before they go on the wall. Create the frame as you attach each piece to the wall. This installation method allows the Peg-Board to float off the wall, making room for the hooks to fit properly in the holes.

5. Once the frame is installed, you can screw the Peg-Board to the frame using the ¾-inch wood screws. Be sure to screw all four corners and then screw it in two equidistant places on all four sides. Avoid those spots where the frame is screwed into the wall.

6. Add the Peg-Board hooks and holders, and hang up your tools and supplies.

Screwing into Drywall and Masonry

With the right bits, screws, and anchors you can drill into any wall in your house. If you're drilling into drywall, use a standard twist bit. If you're drilling into masonry or plaster, use a masonry bit. Similarly, use the right type of screw for the surface you're working with: a wood screw for drywall studs and a masonry screw for masonry or plaster walls.

As I mentioned in step 3 of the Peg-Board project, if the placement of your object necessitates using anchors because screws do not meet up with wall studs, you need to install anchors in the wall before attaching the rack with screws. There are several different kinds of wall anchors, the two most common being expansion anchors and hollow wall anchors. They can be made of plastic or metal.

An expansion anchor is used when going into solid material, such as concrete or masonry. An expansion anchor is installed by drilling a hole in the wall large enough to accommodate it snugly when tapped into the hole using a mallet or hammer covered with a rag to protect the surface of the wall. The expansion anchor expands in diameter as the screw is screwed into it.

The size of the hole you drill depends on the size of the anchor. Furthermore, different sizes of anchors accommodate different size screws. Confused? Don't be. Choose anchors and screws according to the weight of the board and the tools it will be carrying. In the example of the Peg-Board tool storage rack, for example, if you are attaching the Peg-Board frame to masonry or plaster, use an expansion anchor designed to hold up to 50 pounds of weight each. That amount of holding power should be sufficient to carry a variety of power and hand tools. Here's how.

1. Put on safety glasses. Once you have determined where the screws need to go, drill a hole using a masonry bit to fit the particular diameter and length of the extension anchor. A masonry bit has a tungsten-carbide tip, a strong coating that allows it to cut through masonry. When drilling into a masonry wall, I recommend operating the power drill at the highest speed and backing it out frequently to pull out masonry debris and dust that will clog the hole and overheat the drill.

2. Insert the anchor in the hole and tap it flush with the wall using a mallet or hammer covered with a rag to protect the surface of the wall. Repeat the process with the remaining anchors.
3. Predrill holes in the object you want to hang, if necessary, to match up with the anchors you have placed in the wall. Insert standard screws of the appropriate size for the anchors into the holes and tighten. Hang the object.

A hollow wall anchor is used when attaching an item to drywall. They are designed to spread out behind the drywall and hold screws firmly in place.

In our Peg-Board example, if you are attaching the Peg-Board frame to drywall, use hollow-wall anchors designed to hold up to 50 pounds of weight each.

1. Put on safety glasses. Once you have determined where the screws need to go, drill a hole using a standard twist bit to fit the particular diameter and length of the hollow wall anchor.
2. Insert the anchor in the hole and tap it flush with the wall using a mallet or hammer covered with a rag to protect the surface of the wall. Repeat the process with the remaining anchors.
3. Predrill holes in the object you want to hang, if necessary, to match up with the anchors you have placed in the wall. Insert screws into the holes and tighten. Hang the object.

There's No Such Thing as Too Many Tools: A Glossary

It's frustrating to go to a home center or local hardware store only to be faced with aisles of gadgets, gizmos, instruments, and implements and have no idea what they are or how they work. Right here, right now, I'll demystify the wild and wonderful world of tools. This glossary will enable you to confidently go to the store and ask for—and get—what you need!

GET A GRIP!

Bench vise

Clamps are incredibly useful items to have: They can take the place of an AWOL teenager, a busy friend, or a snoring spouse. And they don't talk back, either. Clamps steady things you are working on, or they secure glued items together while they dry.

A bench vise and a counter or tabletop are all you need to hold an unwieldy piece of wood awaiting drilling or to act as a temporary vise on the edge of a workbench. Small spring clamps will hold veneer in place while glue is setting it permanently. They can even hold a slippery trash bag to a barrel or secure a canvas drop cloth to an outdoor worktable on a windy day. More specialized clamps perform other exciting miracles of holding power!

I recommend buying an inexpensive clamp-on bench vise with 4-inch jaws. You can either temporarily attach this to a kitchen counter, workbench, or table and then store it away when it's not in use, or you can clamp it to a worktable and leave it there. Attach the vise to one end of your table instead of the middle of the table to leave yourself most of the table length to work.

C-clamp

Two 3-inch C-clamps will handle almost any household project. A C-clamp holds work between a pad, which often swivels, and an anvil. Turning the spindle adjusts the grip. C-clamps are very inexpensive and versatile.

Corner clamp

This highly specialized clamp is perfect for holding mitered or picture frame corners together. It holds two pieces together at a 90-degree angle. Corner clamps often feature a saw slot for cutting 45-degree angles.

Spring clamps

Spring clamps come in a variety of sizes and are made of either metal or plastic. They are perfect for holding thinner materials and useful for craft projects and small repair jobs. The plastic ones are not as sturdy as the metal ones. Either way, they're inexpensive, so it is worth having a set of them in various sizes.

Web clamp

Woodworkers mainly use web clamps to hold several wide pieces of wood that have been glued together. However, web clamps also have some application for anyone who is faced with a wobbly chair that needs regluing or a cabinet that needs to be held in place while each of its four sides are nailed together. This clamp is made up of a long and very sturdy nylon strap that can be wrapped around any item you are working on. A ratchet device tightens and holds the strap in place. Web clamps are expensive, though, so you can use a bungee cord to approximate the function of a web clamp.

Slip joint pliers

This gripping tool has two hinged arms and serrated jaws for better holding power. The movable joint allows the tool to adjust to two positions, one with a wider open position. Slip joint pliers can be used for a variety of holding tasks in woodworking, general repair, and plumbing jobs—even craft projects. For example, you can more easily get a stubborn nut off of a bolt with slip joint pliers.

Adjustable wrench

The opening of this wrench adjusts by rotating a threaded adjuster with your thumb. What's great about an adjustable wrench is that you can change the size of the opening by millimeters, allowing you to hold or turn a variety of different-size objects. It's especially useful if you are adjusting the height of a bicycle, for example. Adjustable wrenches come in a wide variety of sizes. I recommend the 8 inch or 12-inch size for most household tasks, but they also come in 6-inch and 10-inch models.

Cable ties

Cable ties are lengths of sturdy plastic with an opening at the end that lets you slip the opposite end through it and pull it tight for a very strong grip. They come in a variety of lengths, from 4 inches to 48 inches, and lots of great colors. Cable ties can hold glued items together while the glue dries (you need to cut cable ties with a sturdy pair of scissors or snips). Cable ties are also great for tying up recycled newspapers and cardboard or for holding several computer or electronic wires together to keep them neat.

CUT IT UP

Diagonal cutting pliers

These handy little clippers cut wire easily, and you may find them useful for other wire-cutting tasks as well. A standard 7-inch model is the most versatile for doing simple electrical repairs.

Metal snips

Snips look like scissors with stubby blades. They are used for cutting sheet metal, but they also come in handy for cutting chicken wire, screening, steel strapping, and other metal items. Don't use metal snips to cut electrical wire: The wire can nick the blades and leave a ragged edge on your next cutting project.

Utility knife

Utility knives are versatile because of their convenient size and retractable and replaceable *extremely sharp* blades. You can buy inexpensive plastic ones, but I recommend you get a good-quality retractable utility knife. (It still won't be very expensive.) Always be sure to have extra blades on hand because you will want to change them often; a dull blade is dangerous. For general cutting, use a standard single-edged reversible blade. When one side gets dull, you can turn it around and use the other side. Just in case you get the urge to replace your kitchen floor, a scoring blade, which can be put into the same metal knife, can be used for cutting linoleum and vinyl.

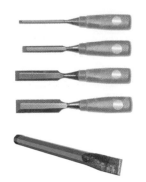

Wood and cold chisels

There are many different kinds of wood chisels, but most household chiseling jobs can be accomplished with a basic set of four that will come in ¼-, ½-, ¾-, and 1-inch sizes. The better the quality of chisel set, the sharper and more precise the edge. You can use wood chisels to cut out a recess (often known as a mortise) for door hinges and other hardware. Cold chisels aren't as sharp as wood chisels and are used on masonry. *Always wear safety glasses when working with a chisel.*

A BIT ABOUT DRILLS AND SCREWS

Allen wrenches or hex keys

The little screws with no heads that often come with flat pack assemble-it-yourself furniture are called "setscrews." You need an Allen wrench, sometimes known as a hex key, to put them in or remove them. Flat pack furniture often comes with a small Allen wrench, but it's handy to have a set of Allen wrenches in your tool kit because chances are as soon as you finish putting that TV stand together the Allen wrench that came with it will fall into a black hole never to return. When you want to disassemble any furniture that is put together with setscrews, you will have the needed tool on hand. You can buy larger Allen wrenches individually if need be. They are very affordable.

Power and cordless drills

A power drill with variable speeds is truly a must-have in every home, especially if it reverses. A close cousin to the power drill is the cordless drill, which runs on rechargeable batteries. Cordless drills have a tendency not to be as powerful as power drills, but they are certainly handy and don't encumber you with a cord. They do weigh more than power drills because the battery pack is at the base of the drill.

I developed a battery-powered drill that has a separate battery pack that is attached to the drill with a flexible cord. It hooks onto the waist of your pants, making the drill itself lighter.

Your ability to get into tight spaces or do drilling jobs outside is enhanced with a cordless drill. You charge the battery pack by plugging it in overnight according to the manufacturer's instructions. Most power and cordless drills have a built-in tightening mechanism, making it easy to switch bit sizes and types.

Drill bits

You can buy drill bits in a variety of sizes, usually in convenient sets. Bits fit into both power and cordless drills and are standard in size, so you do not have to worry about matching brands. Twist bits are good for predrilling holes for screws and come in sizes to complement a whole range of screw sizes. Spade bits and paddle bits are good for drilling large holes. (For example, you'd use one of these bits to drill a larger hole in the back of an armoire that you are converting into a television or stereo cabinet so that plugs and wires can easily fit through it.) Masonry bits drill into concrete walls. They have tungsten-carbide tips that will not dull when penetrating such hard material. Ceramic tile bits, which look like little spades, are perfect for drilling through glass and china. (You'd use this bit if you wanted to make a clock out of a pretty plate you found at a flea market. A ceramic tile bit will allow you to drill the proper hole through the middle so you can attach the clock works.)

Electric and cordless screwdrivers

An electric screwdriver can make driving screws easier than a manual screwdriver can, and it's lighter than a reversible drill. It makes light, simple work of basic screwing tasks.

Flat head screwdrivers

Flat head screwdrivers can sometimes be frustrating. Unless you match the size of the head with the slot in the screw, it will easily slip out and end up "stripping" the screw, which means that the soft metal of the screw will become nicked, widened, and generally damaged and useless. So it's important to have a good set of flat head screwdrivers in a variety of sizes, from small to large.

You can also invest in a magnetic tip ratchet screwdriver. The handle stays the same, and you can change heads or bits just as you would with a drill. These take up less room than a set of screwdrivers. But it is handy to have the variety of lengths a set of individual screwdrivers can offer—from the very tiny to the very large.

Nut drivers

Nut drivers are like screwdrivers, except they drive nuts, of course! You can also buy nut driver bits or heads designed to fit into an electric drill/screwdriver. Buy a set of four or five nut driver heads that range in size from ¼ inch to 1 inch.

Phillips head screwdrivers

A Phillips head screwdriver has a little cross at the top of it, as does the screw itself. There is more flexibility in matching head to screw with a Phillips head because the cross allows the driver to grip the screw more tightly than does a flat head screwdriver.

6-in-1 screwdriver

A 6-in-1 screwdriver is a powerhouse of versatility and function. It offers two double-ended screwdriver bits, one double-ended nut/bolt driver, and one standard screwdriver grip/handle that provide the most commonly used sizes of flat head and Phillips head screwdrivers as well as nut/bolt drivers in one handy tool.

WIRE WORK

Long nose pliers

If you have ever made a beaded necklace or any kind of jewelry, you very well may have used long nose or finer needle nose pliers. A 7- or 8-inch pair will allow you to form loops in wires or to get into tight spaces to grab the end of a wire (or other small items).

Wire stripper

This strange-looking implement easily takes the plastic coating off of most covered wires, and it will also measure the size of wire and crimp the end of a wire or terminal. A wire stripper is really essential if you are planning on doing a lot of simple electrical work around the house. Trying to strip a small wire with a knife can be frustrating *and* dangerous.

Receptacle tester

This gadget plugs into any outlet and tells you if electrical wires are alive or dead without passing on a shock to you. The little lights on the top of the tester give you the information you need. A receptacle tester is easy and safe to use and very inexpensive, and it can save you time when you are troubleshooting or diagnosing electrical wire problems.

Neon circuit tester

This very handy tool can quickly indicate whether it is safe to touch a wire without your actually having to touch it. All you have to do is hold one of the two probes to a metallic box or bare wire and the other to the wire in question. If the bulb at the top of the neon circuit tester glows, you have a "hot" or "live" wire.

NAILING IT!

Curved claw hammer

Don't be put off by the somewhat scary name: Usually, people call this most useful of tools simply a hammer. That's because while there are several different kinds of hammers, this one is the most versatile and can perform most hammering and nail removal tasks you will face around the house.

A hammer's head drives nails into place, and its claw end pries out nails. It can also be used for other prying jobs. Despite the fact that claw hammers are easily found, they come in a variety of sizes, so choose one that feels good in your hand and isn't too big for you to wield forcefully without struggling. A 10-ounce version is good for many household repairs. But you can also find 13- and 16-ounce hammers, which are good for woodworking projects. A 16-ounce hammer may be too bulky for a lot of women, but you never know. Try all three and see which one is best for you.

Mallet

A mallet looks like a large judge's gavel, only with a rubber head. They are lighter than standard metal hammers. Mallets are very useful for pounding objects you don't want to dent or break, such as the joints of wood furniture or a slab of flagstone. Mallets can be used to put forceful pressure behind anything that a metal hammer's head would

damage because the concentrated force of a small hammer head is greater than the force of the larger surface of the rubber mallet. Mallets are not very expensive, and they are worth having on hand.

> **SAFETY NOTE**
>
> Remember: Always use safety glasses when hammering!

Nail set

Nail sets are useful for any woodworking project because they help drive the nail a bit below the surface you have nailed, allowing you to fill the space with wood filler and stain or paint over the nail, rendering it invisible. The nail set should be slightly smaller than the nail you have used, which is why it's a good idea to buy a couple of nail sets, a small one and a medium-sized one. That way you can set small brads as well as larger nails.

To use a nail set, simply hammer in the nail until the head just reaches the surface, then place the appropriate-sized nail set in the center of the nail and tap the top of it with your hammer until the nail is just slightly below the surface of the wood. Using your finger, patch the small hole with some wood filler.

Pry bar

Sometimes the claw of a hammer just isn't long enough to give you the leverage that

you need to pry a nail or other object away from the surface it's attached to. That's where a pry bar comes in. The pry bar's length gives you the leverage you need to put pressure on one end to remove especially stubborn nails or screws. A 12-inch pry bar should be sufficient for most jobs.

Staple gun

No woman should be without her gun—her staple gun, that is! Staple guns perform so many tasks, from re-covering the seat of a simple side chair to affixing latticework to a garden fence. Depending on the kind of staples you use, your gun can move easily from indoors to out. You can still buy standard manual staple guns, but power electric or cordless guns are now available and are powerful yet easier to use. And some staple guns also allow you to switch over from staples to small brads, making light nailing jobs even easier.

Tack hammer

Tack hammers have standard handles but narrow heads, usually with a magnet on one side for holding tacks and brads. Upholsterers use tack hammers for tacking fabric, padding, and lining to furniture and for driving decorative nail heads into furniture for a decorative and practical touch. Because a tack hammer is small and easy to control, it's also good for finer nailing jobs such as repairing a picture frame, where a standard hammer might damage the wood. A tack hammer can also get into tighter spaces than a regular hammer, so if you are hammering something at an odd angle, a tack hammer might be just the thing you need.

HIGHER GROUND

Stepladder

Don't skimp on a ladder. Buy the very best one you can afford, and use it only according to the manufacturer's instructions. Many household repairs and decorating jobs will require elevation of some kind. Please, please, don't use chairs, boxes, or stacks of books to raise yourself up! This is so dangerous. Invest in a good metal or wooden folding stepladder. It slips neatly into a broom closet or under your bed and is light enough to carry from room to room. Stepladders range from 3 to 12 feet. A 6-foot ladder is a good choice for most households, although you may also want to

REACH THE PEAK OF SAFETY

Ladder use requires concentration and care. When working on a ladder, you have to focus both on what you are doing and be conscious that you are on a ladder. That means first and foremost removing all distractions when working on a ladder. Turning your head to answer a child's question or to shoo the cat out of the toolbox could spell disaster when you are balancing on high to hang a curtain rod or paint ceiling trim. That means children, pets, television noise, and anything else that could take your attention away should be kept out of the room you are working in. Here are some other tips that will keep you safe when on higher ground:

- Before placing a ladder, make sure the surface you are placing it on is free of debris and is level.
- Make sure a stepladder is unfolded all the way and the spreaders are completely rigid.
- Never, *ever* stand on the very top of a ladder!
- Keep your hips within the width of the ladder rails. Work from side to side only as far as your arms can reach without shifting your hips outside of the safety zone of the side rails. Never lean left or right out of that area; move the ladder instead.
- When moving your stepladder from place to place, collapse it. Never carry an unfolded ladder.
- Never, *ever* get on a ladder with another person. One person per ladder!

buy a 3-foot ladder for use in the kitchen. It's so much better than balancing on a chair when reaching for items stored high in your upper cabinets. A 6-foot ladder will likely have a shelf for holding paint buckets or tools. Sometimes the shelf has an indentation for a bucket so that it has less of a chance of slipping off the shelf. Look for rugged hinges, a sturdy X brace on the rear legs, and rubber footings that will grip the floor and keep the ladder from moving around.

Extension ladder

An extension ladder is made up of two straight ladders with a brace that allows the user to extend the length. Extension ladders are usually used on larger construction sites and are not really necessary for most household jobs.

Folding ladder

There are two kinds of folding ladders: One is a stepladder that folds so it can be placed on surfaces of different heights, such as the floor and a stair tread. A folding straight ladder is similar to an extension ladder, except that it can also be folded over to resemble a stepladder.

TILE TIME

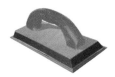

Grout float

A float is a rectangular plate with a handle on top and a rubber pad. It helps spread grout over tiles and stone smoothly and evenly. The rubber pad acts like a squeegee to move and pack the grout in between tiles, and it also wipes away excess grout—all in one fell swoop.

Notched spreader

This is a metal plate with a handle on top, which is notched on two sides. It is used for applying mastic or tile adhesive to somewhat large areas. The notches create ridges in the adhesive for good, even contact with the tile.

Putty knife

Putty knives come in a variety of sizes—from narrow to wide to those used for drywall applications. Putty knives are not really knives at all; they are more like metal spatulas, and you will find they have a variety of uses. For example, in masonry or tiling projects, you can use a putty knife to "butter" the back of small pieces of tile with adhesive to fit in places that a notched spreader will not fit.

Steel trowel

Steel trowels are flat, metal, pie-shaped blades with a handle on one end. They are mainly used to do brickwork and may not be necessary for general household projects.

MEASURING UP

Tape measure

Most household projects require some form of measuring. Accurate measurements are essential to everything from hanging a picture to building a shelf to placing a sofa. Flexible tape measures are handy for most measuring jobs, including calculating circumferences. In fact, I recommend carrying a tape measure with you whenever you are going to a flea market or going furniture shopping so you can measure larger items before you buy them. The best tape measure to have is a metal retractable rule with a lock that allows you to hold it at a certain measure. A 25-foot tape measure is most practical.

Folding ruler

Folding rulers are usually made out of wood. It may seem old-fashioned, but they are still being made, and they are useful. A folding

INCH BY INCH

There are two edges on every tape measure. One edge usually indicates inches divided into 16ths. The scale along the opposite edge has $\frac{1}{32}$-inch graduations for the first 6 or 12 inches. It allows you to mark off very precise measurements.

ruler provides rigidity for measuring where a flexible tape measure might sag or fall over, such as measuring distances straight up over your head or beyond your arm's reach (and when there is no one available to hold the other end of a tape measure). Folding rulers usually unfold by foot lengths up to 6 or 8 feet.

Carpenter's square

This type of ruler is used to draw 90-degree angles more than it is used for measuring. If you are interested in making your own mats for picture frames or if you are planning on trying your hand at some woodworking projects, a carpenter's square is nice to have.

Compass

A compass is a metal device just like the one you used in grade school to draw circles. And that's what you can use it for today! You may want to cut a circle that's larger than what a drill bit can handle, so a compass is a good way of making a perfect round, which you can then cut out with a scroll or saber saw. A compass is also good for scribing around edges that are not completely straight. For example, if you are cut-

ting a piece of vinyl flooring to fit around a doorway, you can scribe the outline of the doorway and transfer it easily to your vinyl for a perfect fit.

Level

A level helps you make sure your lines are straight and is particularly handy when hanging pictures, curtain rods, and shelves. There are several kinds of levels, including technologically advanced laser levels that "shoot" a line of light across an area. Technological advances aside, there are three basic kinds of levels: carpenter's, line, and torpedo levels. Buy a level with both a horizontal and a vertical bubble.

A **carpenter's level** is rectangular and can run anywhere from 18 to 96 inches long! A length somewhere in between those two will be useful for most household projects. Look for a carpenter's level with at least three bubble windows: one in the center for checking level and one on either end for checking if a surface or edge is plumb. Windows that you can look at from above are very useful if you are working on floors or other surfaces where looking from the side would be impossible.

A **line level** is usually short (less than 12 inches) and has one center bubble window. This level has two hooks on either end so it can be attached to a rope. That makes it useful for outdoor projects or when leveling items that are far apart, such as checking for level between fence posts.

A **torpedo level** is short, no more than 9 inches long generally, and has three bubble windows, one in the middle and two flanking either side of the center window.

The compact size of the level makes it useful for checking level of pictures or small areas where a carpenter's level won't fit. Look for a torpedo level that lights up for easy viewing.

Chalk line

Chalk lines mark straight lines for applying molding to walls, laying out garden paths or patios, and a host of other projects that requires marking out long or large areas. A chalk line marker looks like an enclosed fishing reel. It has both reusable string and chalk inside it. You pull it taut, with the help of a friend, and then snap it. Voila! A chalk line will be created. Sometimes chalk line markers have hoods you can attach to a wall or a pole in the ground if extra hands are not available.

THE ART OF PAINTING

Bucket and can pourer

Most hardware and paint stores sell buckets. It's a good idea to pour the paint you are using from its can into a widemouthed paint bucket. Using a bucket instead of the can eliminates drips on the can. When you use paint straight from the can, the ridges in which the paint can lid sits always get filled with paint, making it difficult to get the top on securely when you are done. Hardware stores also sell plastic pouring rims that fit on gallon paint cans, which make pouring into a bucket very neat as well.

Caulking gun

Small caulking jobs such as filling in nail holes in furniture before painting can be done with your finger. But bigger jobs, such as caulking around molding or window frames, should be done with a caulking gun. These are inexpensive, and most caulk is sold in standard-size tubes that fit in caulking guns. If you have never used one before, practice first on newspaper to get a feel for it. The tube fits easily into the gun, and you apply pressure with the trigger. The trigger action automatically pushes a lever forward from the bottom of the tube, making sure the caulk is always pushed up to the top.

Paintbrushes

Paintbrushes come in all shapes and sizes to meet various painting needs. There are sash brushes for painting moldings around windows and doors and large brushes for painting wide, flat areas. There are even small brushes for getting around thin chair legs and other small areas. And paint-

brushes come in a variety of materials, too: foam, nylon, and natural bristle.

Latex paint, which is now commonly used in all household applications because it is water-based, easy to clean up, and more environmentally friendly than oil paint, requires the use of nylon or foam brushes. Natural brushes can only be used with oil paint and can be costly. But many synthetic brushes are now made for use with oil-based or alkyd paints. Foam brushes can be used with latex or acrylic paints and help reduce the appearance of brush strokes.

Even synthetic brushes can be expensive, so if you do invest in a good set of brushes, be sure to clean and dry them after each use and store them with the brush faces up so they do not break or stretch. I recommend buying four good all-purpose synthetic brushes in 1-, 2-, 3-, and 4-inch widths. You can handle any small job with these brushes. Any large job should be done with a roller.

Paint mitts

Paint mitts are a fairly new invention. They are literally mitten-like gloves with palms that are covered in a material similar to a roller. They are useful if you are planning on painting a lot of stair spindles or chair legs, which can be awkward to paint with a flat brush. The idea is to pour paint into a roller tray and put the palm of the glove (while you are wearing it) right into the paint lightly, so as not to drip. Then you can rub your mitted hand up and down the spindle or cylindrical object to paint it.

Paint pads

Paint pads have handles on top and are usually made of foam. They offer very smooth, even coverage over a large flat area. They take a little getting used to, however, and you might be just as well off using a roller for a large painting job.

Paint rollers

Rollers come is a variety of "naps," which are chosen according to the surface you are painting. If you are painting brick, for example, you want a thicker, rougher nap that will help get the paint into all the nooks and crannies of the masonry. If you are painting drywall or plaster, you want a fine nap, which will achieve a smooth finish. If you are painting a large surface, such as a wall or ceiling, a roller is the way to go. Extension handles allow you to go right up a high wall or reach a ceiling with relative ease.

Paint tray and tray liner

Paint trays are made for use with a roller. A light plastic liner is a cheap way to keep the metal tray clean and to keep cleanup to a minimum. When you are done painting, you can simply toss the liner away and wipe out the tray.

Painter's tape

Painter's tape is low-tack tape, meaning that it will not mar surfaces where you apply it to mask out areas where you do not want the paint to go. The tape is usually bright blue, but sometimes it can come in other colors. The adhesive on regular masking tape can stick to paint surfaces or, worse, tear them off when you remove the tape. So if you want to tape off surfaces (for example, around windows and doors before you paint molding), always make sure you are using painter's tape. It is more expensive than regular masking tape, but it's worth the price because it saves having to repaint and repair a wall ruined by masking tape.

Sandpaper and sanders

Sandpaper is useful in the preparation of surfaces to be painted. Sandpaper comes in a variety of grits from very fine to very rough.

Sandpaper is always numbered, and that number indicates the particle size of the grit. The higher the number of the sandpaper, the finer its particles will be and vice versa. Common grit categories and their uses are:

- 12 to 30 grit: very coarse, good for removing thick coats of paint or roughing up a metal or plastic surface to accept a base coat
- 36 to 50 grit: coarse, good for smoothing out surface imperfections on rough wood or for removing rust from metal
- 60 to 100 grit: medium, good for preliminary smoothing of wood surfaces in preparation for painting
- 120 to 180 grit: fine, good for final finishing of bare wood meant to be stained or painted and for sanding between coats of paint on wooded furniture and accessories
- 220 to 600 grit: very fine, good for smoothing and polishing finish paint and stain or polyurethane coats on wood and metal

Use sandpaper as is for small jobs or use a sanding block, electric palm sander, or belt sander for bigger projects. A **sanding block** is easy to handle on medium-sized surfaces, such as a tabletop. An **electric palm sander** is useful for sanding tables and furniture and will be less tiring to use than a block. It's small enough to, like the name says, fit in your hand or palm. A **belt sander** is good for sanding large items such as doors. It's heavier than an electric palm sander, making it more unwieldy to use. You can also get smaller or specialized electric sanders that fit in small spaces.

No matter what kind of sandpaper you use or what kind of device you use it with, sand wood in the direction of the grain; otherwise you will mar the surface, and it will be difficult to repair.

Steel wool comes in similar grades of abrasion as sandpaper and can also be used for sanding purposes. Very fine grits of steel wool, which come in flat, thin pads or the more familiar-looking pillows, can be used for removing, polishing, and cleaning finishes, and for sanding between coats of finish and paint. They are especially useful on furniture projects. Coarse grit steel wool can be used for cleaning rust off metal objects. For example, if you are repainting outdoor metal or wrought-iron furniture, a good scrub with a steel wool pad will remove loose surface rust and prepare the surface for a coat of metal primer.

Paint scraper

You use a paint scraper to prepare wall surfaces for painting. It helps get rid of bumps and dried drips of paint that can prevent you from achieving a smooth look to your new paint job. And remember, in painting as in life, preparation is everything! Most scrapers are made of plastic, but in a pinch you can use a wide metal putty knife to remove any bumps from your wall.

Wallpaper scoring tool

This small, round device has many little blades that score wallpaper for easier removal. The scoring allows water to penetrate the paper and soften the wallpaper paste faster. Simply run the tool in big circles across the wallpapered area and then spray or wet down the wallpaper with a sponge. The wallpaper should, once the glue is softened, scrape off with a little elbow grease. You can also rent a wallpaper steamer, which helps to make short work of wallpaper removal as well.

Wire brush

Wire brushes are good for removing old paint from metal and wood surfaces, especially in hard-to-reach places such as between spindles and chair legs. Be sure to sand the area you brushed with the metal bristle, however, because it can leave little grooves in whatever you have brushed.

TAKE THE PLUNGE

Hand auger

A hand auger is like a snake that spools back into its reel so you don't have to touch it. This is a useful item if you think there is something blocking your sink and the plunger doesn't help. There is a spiral hook at the end of the auger that will push through a grease, soap, or food clog and clear the pipe. To use a hand auger (which may not come with instructions), push the flexible snake into the drain until you feel the

blockage. Tighten the locknut and turn the handle clockwise while pushing on the body. The spiral hook will either loosen the clog and bore through it, or it will grab onto the cause of the stoppage so you can retrieve it.

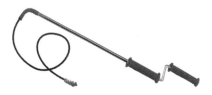

Closet auger

This auger is meant specifically for use in the toilet. (So don't be tempted to use it in the kitchen sink!) It works on the same principle as the hand auger—by moving or fishing out whatever is causing the blockage and clearing a path in the drain.

Pipe wrench

Pipe wrenches are often used in pairs to loosen or tighten pipe connections. That's because you don't want the pipe to turn while you are turning the fitting—because you might not see what the turning pipe is actually affecting inside a wall or beneath the floor. Hold one wrench to keep the pipe in place and use the other wrench to grip and turn the fitting.

Plunger

A good old-fashioned rubber plunger can get rid of most minor sink and toilet clogs. Recommendation: Buy a funnel-cup plunger because they have more power than standard cup plungers. And buy two: one for sink use and the other for toilet use. Do not use a toilet plunger in the sink. That's just not nice!

Spud wrench

This wrench is used for removing or tightening nuts in kitchen and bath fixtures. If you are thinking of replacing old fixtures, a spud wrench will come in handy. Buy an inexpensive, adjustable spud wrench.

SEE SAW

Backsaw and miter box

A backsaw has a rigid spine that stiffens its back, making it fairly inflexible. It is designed to make straight cuts across the grain of wood and is most often used in a miter box. Miter boxes make it very easy to accomplish very straight cuts at 45- or 90-degree angles. That's perfect if you want to make miter cut frames or molding. Miter boxes are made in either wood or plastic, and some have a variety of slots for different angle cuts.

Coping saw

A coping saw is normally used to make fine cuts with sharp curves. Its replaceable blade is flexible, very thin, and extremely sharp. Depending on the blade you use, you can cut wood, plastic, or metal with a coping saw. It's excellent for cutting the scribed edge of molding.

Crosscut saw

A crosscut saw is most useful for cutting wood. As the name implies, it is used most effectively by cutting across the grain of the wood. So, for example, this is a good saw to use to cut lengths of 1×2s or 2×4s. You can also use this saw to cut plywood, which has grain going in both directions.

Hacksaw

Hacksaws are commonly used for cutting through metal, such as a thin pipe. They can also cut through wood and plastic. You can buy blades that range in size from 8 to 12 inches, and the saw adjusts to fit the blade size.

Keyhole saw

Keyhole saws are meant to cut curves and are especially useful when cutting through drywall. Electricians use keyhole saws to cut out holes for pot lights in drywall ceilings, for instance.

Scroll saw

Scroll saws, which are also known as reciprocating saws, saber saws, or jigsaws, are wonderful power saws that are easy to operate with just a little practice. They are extremely useful for all sorts of projects that involve wood. The saw's blade scrolls or rotates at varying speeds, and you can easily cut circular and linear shapes with one. Be-

cause they are so popular, a quality scroll saw can be had at a very reasonable price. The blades are inexpensive enough that you can replace them when they become dull.

There are other power saws, such as chain, table, and circular saws that I did not include on this list. They are dangerous tools that need a certain amount of practice and training before you feel comfortable using them. Many local YMCAs and even some home improvement superstores offer classes in how to use these saws. I urge you to take such a class if you are interested in learning how to use these powerful cutting tools.

SAW SMARTS

No matter what kind of saw you use, these safety tips are always in style:

- Always wear safety glasses when sawing anything, especially when using a power saw.
- Always make straight cuts on the "waste" side of the material, not on the side of the material you will be using.
- Start all cuts on the pull stroke, not the push stroke. This is safer and easier.
- Take long, light stroked with manual saws.
- Take it slow with a power saw.
- Replace or sharpen dull blades. Like dull kitchen knives, dull saw blades are more dangerous than sharp ones!

ETC.
Block plane

A block plane is a wood chisel that is set into a body that allows you to control how much wood is removed from the surface you're working on. This can be used to plane down cabinet or bureau doors that are stuck or even stubborn wooden closet or bedroom doors. Practice makes perfect, however. So I recommend perfecting your technique and control on a scrap piece of wood before you tackle your bulging front door!

Posthole digger and power auger

When you need to dig long, straight holes for fence posts, you need the help of a posthole digger. A shovel, with its wide blade, just won't get the job done. While both manual and power versions make digging deep narrow holes possible, neither one makes hole digging quick and easy. Both tools will give your arms and upper body a workout!

A manual posthole digger, sometimes called a clamshell digger, consists of two long poles with narrow blades on the ends. You plunge the digger into the ground while moving the pole handles in and out. The clamshell-like blades pull the dirt up. This manual digger works well in topsoil that is free of a lot of rocks or tough tree roots, and it's not expensive.

If you need to dig a lot of deep holes in clay or rocky soil, a power posthole digger, also known as a power auger, is for you. In the simplest terms, it's like a wide drill with a motor on top and handles on either side. If you want to use one of these to dig fence-post holes, I recommend renting one. They can be expensive to buy.

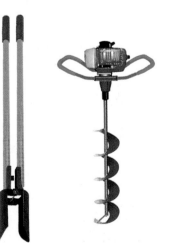

Sawhorses

Two sawhorses are essential equipment if you are going to get serious about home improvement projects. Set up across from each other, two sawhorses can support material you are working on, such as a long piece of wood. Or you can place a piece of plywood or a hollow-core door across them to create a temporary table or workstation. Sawhorses can be bought at any home store. They are made of wood, metal, heavy duty plastic, or a combination of those materials. They can usually be folded up flat for storage.

OPPOSITE: Sawhorses help cut down on the potential messiness of many painting and staining jobs.

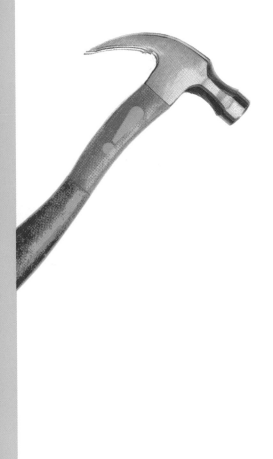

Have Tools, Will Travel

Tools are accessories for living. There are a handful of tools I consider essential for every woman to have: a hammer, pliers, wrench, screwdriver, tape measure, level, and a set of Allen wrenches. If you have those nearby, you are well on your way to home repair victory.

A basic tool kit will include just a few more useful tools and materials. But before you go out and buy everything or anything on the following three lists, check out what you already own. Do you like them? Do they feel good in your hands? Do you want to use them? Keep what you like and what works for you, donate what doesn't (but may be good for someone else), and toss or recycle the rest (anything broken, damaged, rusted, or dull and therefore useless).

Barbara K's Basic Tool Kit

These tools and materials should be part of your household tool arsenal. This may seem like a long list, but many of these items are inexpensive and don't take up a lot of room.

Tools

- Adjustable wrench
- Allen wrenches, or hex keys, in a variety of sizes
- Backsaw and miter box
- Buckets in a range of sizes
- Bungee cords
- Carpenter's square
- C-clamp
- Claw hammer with soft grip
- Compass, or scribe
- Hacksaw
- Level
- Long nose pliers
- Nail set
- Paintbrushes (four to six in a variety of sizes, from small artist brushes to standard wall paint brushes, in both natural bristle and nylon)
- Pipe cutter
- Plunger
- Power drill with additional screwing capability and a set of drill and screw bits
- Pry bar
- Putty knife
- Receptacle tester
- Safety goggles (plastic)
- Sawhorses
- Screwdrivers (four flat heads and four Phillips heads in mini, small, medium, and large) or a 6-in-1 interchangeable screwdriver
- Slip joint pliers
- Spring clamps (small and medium)
- Staple gun with staples

- Step ladder (4 to 6 feet)
- Tape measure (retractable with locking mechanism to hold measures)
- Tweezers (large)
- Utility knife with extra replacement blades
- Wire brush
- Wire stripper
- Wood chisel

Materials
- Cable ties
- Construction adhesive (one brand is called Liquid Nails)
- Duct tape
- Electrical tape
- Extension cords (indoor and outdoor)
- Glue gun and glue sticks
- Nails in a variety of sizes and finishes including metal, brass, and galvanized
- Rags (clean and soft)
- Sanding block and sandpaper in various grits
- Screws in a variety of sizes and finishes including metal, brass, and galvanized
- Sponges (both bone-shaped and household size are good for cleanup)
- Spray bottle
- Steel wool in a variety of grades
- Thread sealant tape

- White glue
- Wood filler or putty
- Wood glue

Advanced Tool Kit
Add these items to the list above, and you'll have an awesome bag of tricks up your sleeve!

Tools
- Bench vise
- Block plane
- Caulking gun
- Chalk line
- Closet auger
- Cold chisel
- Combination square
- Coping saw
- Crosscut saw
- Diagonal cutting pliers
- Electric sander with various grades of sandpaper
- Funnel cup plunger
- Grout float
- Hand auger
- Keyhole saw
- Knee pads
- Mallet
- Metal snips or metal shears
- Neon circuit tester
- Notched spreader
- Nut driver
- Pipe wrench
- Scroll or reciprocating power saw
- Sledge hammer
- Spud wrench

- Steel trowel
- Stud finder (Unfortunately, this won't help you find a man, but it will impress one if you know how to use it!)
- Tack hammer
- Web clamps

Materials
- Paint pad
- Paint roller with rolls
- Paint scraper
- Paint tray
- Painter's tape
- Wallpaper scoring tool

Optional but Fabulous Tools!
This dream team list of special tools is fantastic to own, but these tools are not necessary for the repairs in this book. But they sure would be fun to have, especially if you are thinking of doing larger or more ambitious restoration or woodworking projects inside the house and out in your yard or surrounding landscape.

- Bench vise
- Chain saw
- Laser level
- Locking C-clamp
- Pneumatic nail gun
- Pointing tool
- Router table
- Router and bits
- Soldering gun and solder
- Table saw

Chapter 2
The Walls Around You

Walls, whether they're made from drywall, plaster, wood, stone, or masonry, represent something that both surrounds and divides us. Walls are a huge part of life; they provide privacy and shelter no matter where you are—at home, in the office, even when you're on vacation. Think about what goes into making a wall: There's a great deal of intricacy in the building of a stone wall, for instance. And even the simplest sheet of interior drywall won't stay up without the assistance of the studs and tracks that support it.

Walls and ceilings offer the most opportunities for simple yet dramatic change. By enhancing walls with any of the finishes available—from paint to wallpaper—and embellishing them with artwork and photographs, you can make a space your own, express your style, and display what makes you happy. In doing this, you will completely transform a room.

Even better: Wall and ceiling projects are among the easiest of home improvement and decorating jobs to accomplish. Best of all? Most wall and ceiling fixes will give you immediate results, helping to build your confidence to take on more challenging projects.

SAFETY NOTES

Remember to always follow the manufacturer's instructions when using any product, even if you have used it in the past. Manufacturers take a lot of time to write user-friendly instructions, and they know better than anyone how to use their particular materials or tools. Also remember when embarking on any wall or ceiling project to work in a room that's been cleared of any breakable or moving objects. (That means no Limoges vases or Rollerblades, please.)

If you can't move a piece of furniture because it's too big, cover it with a drop cloth to protect it. Even if you are working in a small area, protect adjacent surfaces or move them out of the way. That kind of preparation can save future heartbreak. You don't want to repair or paint a wall only to find that you've dropped spackling compound on your sideboard.

When working with paint and spackling materials, always work in a well-ventilated room. Keep windows and doors open! Wear a mask if you are kicking up a lot of dust, for example sanding down plaster patches. Wear safety glasses if you are working on your ceiling or with any material that spatters. Clean up and dispose of chemicals, paint, plaster, and other materials according to the manufacturers' recommendations. And please follow your local environment rules for product disposal.

The Pleasure of Paint

Painting is a relatively easy and quick way of breathing new life into a room. The key to achieving a professional look on your own, however, is preparation. Taking a little extra time to ready a room for painting will pay off big time once you get started. And learning about the different kinds of paint and the kind of effects they can achieve is essential. There are so many ways to achieve paint finishes available these days, and each one will result in a different mood, texture, and reflective quality.

I love colors, and luckily there are many of them to choose from today. If you don't like the million plus paint chips in the store, you have the option of bringing in your favorite sweater or skirt, comforter, or vintage image for a computer color match. The creative options are endless. And once you have painted a room, believe me, you'll be bitten by the home improvement bug forever.

I'll spare you the scientific details of paint composition. Basically, paint is a combination of color (pigment) and a binder that allows it to be spread evenly on a surface. But there are certain terms you should know because they will help you choose the right paint for the project.

BEFORE YOU SHOP FOR PAINT

There's nothing I hate more than trekking back to the hardware store for another can of paint because I didn't buy enough in the first place. Measuring the surfaces you are planning on painting will eliminate annoying extra trips to the paint department. It's a simple process, but don't worry if you wind up with a bit more paint than you need. It's smart to have extra paint on hand for touch-ups later on. For example, if you have to repair a patch in a wall, you'll be able to repaint it easily with the leftovers you have on hand.

The surface you will be painting, its condition and original color, as well as the type of paint you want to use will have an impact on the quantity of paint you will need. The basic rule is 1 gallon of paint per 350 to 400 square feet of wall space. However, if you are going from a dark color to a light color, or vice versa, you will likely have to buy a tinted primer in the same quantity. Using a tinted primer will usually allow you to get away with only one coat of paint. But if you are painting a room a very dark color, say a deep red or midnight blue, you may have to use a tinted primer *and* double the amount of paint and then give it two or three coats to get the true, deep color you're after.

Paint Types

Here are the basic types of paint you're likely to encounter.

ACRYLIC: Acrylic paint is a water-based paint commonly used in small painting jobs and craft projects. You can buy it in small bottles in the craft store. It's excellent for painting small details on furniture and accessories. If you find a color of acrylic paint you love, you can have the paint store make a match with latex paint.
Brush fuss: Use synthetic or foam brushes.

LATEX: Latex paint is popular for its ease of use. Latex paints are water-based and have low fumes. Cleanup can be done with liquid soap and water. And dried paint can usually be peeled off of a paint bucket and roller tray surfaces and simply thrown away. Manufacturers have improved the quality and durability of latex paints over the years for indoor and outside applications. Just be sure you are buying interior or exterior grade paint. You might choose to use gloss latex in bathroom and kitchen applications because it has protective water-resistant qualities.
Brush fuss: Use synthetic or foam brushes.

OIL-BASED: Oil-based or alkyd paint is thick and sticky, making it somewhat difficult to work with. Oil paint also has a strong smell. You absolutely must work in a well-ventilated room when working with any oil-based product. It also requires special products for cleanup, such as paint thinner (another smelly and often dangerous chemical). Because manufacturers have made such great strides in latex paint quality and durability, I don't think you need to use oil paint for most jobs. But gloss oil paints, which were commonly used in kitchens and baths because of their water-resistant quality, have a sheen and reflective quality that gloss latex paint just can't match. So if you are dead set on a certain finish (we'll talk about paint finishes in detail later in this chapter), oil gloss may be the only way to go.

You can also buy oil paints formulated for use on hot surfaces, such as ovens, exposed hot water pipes, and radiators (but make sure the products are heat-resistant). Many spray paints are made specifically for appliances, as well. And there are oil-based paints suitable for painting over tile and porcelain that simulate a ceramic finish. The upside to oil paint is its durability, especially on window trim and in kitchens and bathrooms. Today's oil paint is easier to clean, and newer formulations make it less likely to yellow over time.
Brush fuss: Use natural-bristle brushes.

BARBARA'S BEST-KEPT SECRET

If you are doing a painting job over a weekend and using oil paint, you can wait until the very end to clean up the brushes with paint thinner by using this simple mid-process storage trick. Wrap the paintbrushes in aluminum foil, place them in a plastic storage bag, and put the whole thing in the freezer. The brushes will stay pliant, and the paint won't freeze. You can go right back to painting and then clean the brushes out when the job is completely done!

BARBARA'S BEST-KEPT SECRET

The only paint finish that you can spot retouch successfully is flat. When retouching shinier finishes, from eggshell to high gloss, you will need to repaint the entire area surrounding the imperfection. Otherwise, you will see the retouched spot because glossier finishes never spot-dry in a uniform manner.

SPRAY PAINT: Spray paint is oil-based and perfect for painting garden furniture, wrought iron, and just about anything that's made of metal. They even make spray paint that will cover plastic without peeling. Spray paint is easy to use and does not require the prep work that oil paint in a can demands.

PRIMER: Primer is used to prepare surfaces for paint. "Raw" drywall needs to be covered with drywall primer before paint goes on top. Primer basically readies the drywall to accept paint. Primer can also be used when going from a dark to a light color or vice versa. In those cases, you want to ask your paint mixer to create a tinted primer with a color close to but not exactly like the topcoat. This will reduce the number of coats you have to give your wall or ceiling. Primer is also essential if you are covering an oil-based paint with a latex paint. A latex primer will create a suitable surface for the new covering. If you leave out that step, the latex paint will pull right off the oil-based surface. Ugh!

You don't always have to use primer: If you are painting flat beige or off-white walls, you can generally go right over the paint with your new color. One more thing: If you are using spray paint to cover old metal, buy spray paint rustproofing primer to cover the cleaned surface before you put on the paint.

Paint Finishes

These are the different types of paint finishes you have to choose from.

FLAT: This matte surface paint finish is usually used on interior walls. It helps hide small imperfections because it doesn't reflect light. (Shinier paint highlights bumps, dents, and patches.) Flat paint is generally hard to clean or scrub, but some manufacturers are making flat paints that are more easily washable. Still, you have to be cautious when going after scuffs and dirt on a flat-painted wall.

EGGSHELL: This finish has just a whisper of sheen. You could hardly call it shiny. It's good for interior walls, especially if you have kids running around, simply because you will have an easier time cleaning it than a flat-painted wall. However, an eggshell finish still looks somewhat matte, and any imperfections will remain subtle if not invisible.

SATIN: This smooth, somewhat shiny paint is perfect for children's rooms because it's so easy to clean. Kitchens, bathrooms, and high-traffic areas will also benefit from satin finish paints because they hold up under light scrubbing.

SEMIGLOSS: Semigloss paint is most often used on doors, trim, and cabinets in kitchens and bathrooms. It's easy to keep clean, and its subtle shine is rich looking and especially crisp on trim when set against a flat-painted wall. Surface preparation is important, though, because semigloss will show imperfections. So be sure to fill all holes and gouges, smooth surfaces, and sand trim to be painted. Get rid of built-up paint layers and dried drips, too.

GLOSS: Gloss paints are super-shiny. Most people don't use them on interiors, although I have seen ceilings in gloss, and the reflection is amazing. Light bounces off a gloss-painted ceiling, adding a glamorous feel to a room. But that's a daring and very modern look, so know what you are getting into before you go for gloss! Gloss can also look very fresh on bead board wainscoting and on cabinets, trim, and furniture, especially in contemporary settings. A front door painted in high gloss looks stylish and formal, especially when done in a dark color such as forest green or even black. A warning: Gloss paint highlights every surface imperfection, so be sure your plaster or drywall surface is completely smooth before using a high-gloss paint.

Other Paint Terms

These are two more paint terms you need to know to be a painting pro.

CUTTING IN: This simply means painting around doors, windows, molding, and baseboards with an appropriate brush. After you've completed cutting in, you do the rest of the wall-painting job with a roller.

KEY: This slight roughness to a surface allows it to accept paint. For example, if you are planning on painting over a glossy surface, even if it's with more glossy paint, you have to prime it first to give the surface *key*, which will accept the new paint. Otherwise, the paint will peel off.

What Color Is Your Paint Can?

I love color! It can bring such joy and energy to your surroundings. But with so many colors to choose from, how will you know if a color, which may look pretty under the florescent glare of the hardware store lights, is really right for you? You won't, unless you buy a sample and test it on a piece of scrap material (drywall, wood, brick, or stone) that's been primed the same way as the surface you're intending to paint. A paint chip just doesn't cut it when it comes to seeing how a color will act once it's covering all four walls. Some paint manufacturers even offer sample bottles to cover a 2- by 2-foot area of wall, or you can take home a quart of color.

Here's a great way to pinpoint your favorite shade. Buy one sample pot in three shades of the same color: one light, one medium, and one dark. Once you get your samples on the wall, live with them for a week. Check the room at various times of day to see how the color has changed. Do you still like it? Which tones do you like

The same color can be mixed in different tones. Try more than one shade of your chosen color before you make a final decision.

best? Also keep in mind when you will be most using the room you're painting. During the day? At night? Those are the times of day to pay the most attention to how the color looks.

The next consideration is the type of surface you'll be painting, whether it be drywall, plaster, brick, or stone. There is not a lot of difference between painting plaster and drywall surfaces. "Raw" or unfinished drywall needs to be primed before it is painted. Other than that, painting drywall is a breeze. (Follow the directions in the "Paint a Wall" project on page 35.) Painting plaster is the same as painting drywall. And if you have a newly plastered wall, it is important to prime it first (just as you would with brand new drywall) to prepare the surface for a topcoat of paint. It's also a good idea to prime patches before repainting, otherwise the patch color may not match the rest of the wall.

Masonry can be painted with latex paint, but some preparation is required. Brick or stone must be cleaned with a stiff wire brush, and any dust has to be removed with the long hose of a vacuum cleaner or Shop-Vac before painting. Missing grout has to be repaired. The surface has to be primed with a self-sealing primer and then painted with either a thick nap roller (to get into all the nooks and crannies) or a large brush to work the paint into the surface further. Expect to do two coats.

Here's a masonry-painting trick that you may not have thought of: Instead of painting the outside of your fireplace, consider painting the inside of it with a heat resistant, flat, black, oil-based paint made specifically to endure temperatures up to 1000°F (available at any home improvement or paint store). The black paint will make soot invisible. When the fireplace is not in use, the black interior lessens the empty appearance of the firebox. It's sleek and elegant!

My firebox went from gloomy to glamorous with just a lick of paint!

Get Inspired!
Create an Inspiration Board
Time: About 1 hour

Before you paint and decorate a room, create an inspiration board. It will help sort out your thoughts and inspire you to create new color and style combinations. It's a useful decorating tool that's super easy and fun to make.

What You Need
Magazines and books, photos, or other images
Paint chips
Fabric, carpet, and tile samples, if applicable
Glue stick or glue gun and glue
Foam core board (available at craft stores)

How to Get It Done
1. Let it rip! Go through your favorite decorating magazines and catalogs and clip out any pictures you love. It can be a photo of an entire interior, a piece of furniture or an accessory, a texture (think wood floor), or even a color! A favorite photo of the beach or fall leaves can inspire a room. Collect fabric and swatches, paint chips, and carpet samples; you can even pick up tile samples. Gather them together, and chances are you will see a pattern of colors and styles emerge.
2. Next, lay out the clippings, samples, and swatches in the general order of the room. Glue the carpet sample or photo on the bottom of the foam core board. Then attach fabric samples and furniture and accessory images in the middle of the board. Paint chips can be glued in a fan next to furnishings. Attach drapery material or images near the top of the board. This will give you a much clearer idea than sticking samples randomly over the board. Inspirational photos can be stuck to the sides. Try cutting out extra pieces of foam core and sticking images on them to create a 3-D effect on your board. This three-dimensional quality will give life to your collage.
3. Take this board with you when you shop for your room. It will keep you focused and on track. Make one for every room in your house!

OPPOSITE: An inspiration board is a great way to organize your ideas and keep your decorating project focused.

BARBARA'S BEST-KEPT SECRET

Don't paint on a humid or rainy day. Humidity is the enemy of drying paint.

Prepping for Painting

Okay. You've selected a dreamy color and bought it in just the right amount. Now you're ready to plunge in and make some changes. First things first: your outfit. Wear comfortable clothes you don't care about because you will, *I guarantee*, get paint on your shirt, pants, and shoes, which could become your new fashion statement. A well-worn T-shirt, old jeans, and dirty sneakers with good rubber soles are appropriate choices.

Next clear out the room you will be painting and cover any surfaces you can't move. Consolidate pictures, books, lamps, accessories, and other small items into a bin so they don't go missing. Move heavy furniture into the center of the room if you can't take it out of the space. Cover all remaining items, and the floor, with drop cloths. Inexpensive plastic drop cloths are perfect for covering furniture, but they are not good for protecting the floor because they are slippery. *Do not cover the floor with a plastic drop cloth!* Use a heavy-duty canvas drop cloth for the floor. Canvas drop cloths are not expensive, and they last forever.

Once your room is cleared and protected, remove everything you can from the walls. Unscrew switch plate covers, drapery hardware, and doorknobs. If you don't want to take off the doorknob, tape off the knob *completely* with masking tape. Keep all the bits and pieces in a plastic storage bag and place it in your accessory bin. Then tape off the moldings with painter's tape. It's low tack and won't rip off paint when you remove it.

Open the doors and windows. Even if it's cold outside, put on a sweatshirt and open windows at least a crack, just to keep fresh air flowing in the room. The point is not to close off the room. Any fumes will be reduced and the room will dry faster.

Go around the room and fill any small holes and cracks with joint compound. It's easy: Using a putty knife or even your finger, spread the joint compound into the small hole or crack. (We'll talk about bigger holes later in this chapter.) When the compound is dry, sand it down until it's smooth. Better yet, instead of sanding, use the contractor's trick of gently rubbing the spot with a damp sponge in a circular motion. This will cut down on the texture that sandpaper can sometimes create, leaving you with a less visible repair.

Use a scraper to remove any bumps or dried paint drips. While you are waiting for the spackle to dry (no more than 30 minutes), gather your materials together and place them in one easy-to-reach-for area.

Put Some Color in Your Life, Starting with Your Walls
Paint a Wall

Time: At least 1 full day to an entire weekend, depending on the size and intricacy of the job

Painting a room can take a good chunk of time but it's such a simple, satisfying project that I hope you'll try it. And don't do beige—experiment with a favorite light, happy color or a warm romantic tone. It's worth taking a chance on color because it's a snap to paint over if you don't like it at the end. Chances are, after you live with your choice for a week, you'll love it!

What You Need

Painter's tape

Bins for storage

Drop cloths

Primer

Appropriate rollers and brushes (rough nap rollers for textured or stucco walls, fine nap for drywall and smooth plaster walls, 1- to 2-inch angled-tip brushes for trim, 3- to 4-inch straight-tip brushes for walls)

Flat head screwdriver

Stir sticks (free at the paint store with purchase—ask for extras!)

Paint

Nail

Hammer

Plastic paint bucket or roller paint trays with liners

Extension pole for rollers

Ladder (stepladder or 8-foot ladder)

Razor blade or utility knife

Rags and sponges

Paint thinner, a mask, and rubber gloves (if using oil paint)

How to Get It Done

1. Once the walls are prepared, surfaces not to be painted are covered with painter's tape, accessories are stored in bins, and furniture still in the room is covered with drop cloths. Prime the wall if necessary using both a brush and a roller. Cut in

around doors and windows and around trim moldings. Remember, you only have to prime if you are going from one color extreme to another or if you are moving from an oil-based paint to a latex paint. Primer doesn't take long to dry—about an hour. Test it first, however, before applying the finish coat.

2. Open your paint can with a flat head screwdriver and stir the paint from the bottom using a paint stir stick. I make small holes around the rim by piercing it with a nail and hammer. It might seem like this would allow the paint to spill, but the small holes actually allow the poured paint to drip back into the can and reduce the amount of paint that sits and dries in the can's top ridge. Pour the paint into a plastic bucket and/or roller paint tray (lined with a cheap plastic liner you can toss out when you're done).

3. Begin painting with a 3- or 3½-inch brush and cut in around all doors, baseboards, and windows. Don't dip more than one-third of the brush into the paint. Remove excess by tapping the side of the brush on the bucket. Don't wipe it down—that will remove too much paint.

4. A roller will make short work of large expanses of wall. Once you have painted all around woodwork, get your roller ready. Rolling will reduce paintbrush marks and result in a smooth finish. Placing the end of the roller in an expansion pole allows you to reach to the top of the wall without having to get on a ladder. You will need to stand on a ladder to paint around the top of the wall or tape off the ceiling. Whether you are painting large areas with a roller or a brush, paint in a crosshatch or M pattern.

5. When painting trim, go slowly and try to be as precise as possible. Don't worry too much if you get paint on a glass window. It can be easily scraped off with a razor blade or the edge of your utility knife.

6. If you are painting a ceiling, an extension rod will make the job much easier. Use a ladder (check out ladder safety tips in "Reach the Peak of Safety" on page 13) to cut in at least 3 to 4 inches where the ceiling meets the wall. Then complete the job with a roller on an extension pole. Instead of rolling the paint on a ceiling in an M pattern, use a W pattern. Start at the outside edge of the ceiling and work your way up and down the length of the room. Take breaks; even with a long pole, painting a ceiling is tough on your neck and shoulders. Use a damp rag or sponge to quickly wipe up any paint splatters.

Enjoy the process. Be mindful of what you're doing. With every stroke of the brush, every turn of the roller, you are improving your room and your life. Just think how much better you'll feel in a room full of color, color that you picked out and that you put on the walls yourself.

Wait at least 48 hours after painting a wall before putting anything on your newly painted walls, to ensure that everything is completely dry. Keep the drop cloth down so any paint or water drops can dry. Then fold it up and store it away.

Finally, don't put off cleanup! Clean the rim of the paint can first, before replacing the lid. Cover any remaining paint in the can with a piece of plastic wrap. This will hinder the formation of a "skin." If there is only a small amount of paint left, pour it into a smaller container, such as a glass jar with a tight fitting lid, and mark it with the paint's brand name, color, and number.

Good brushes will last forever if you clean them properly. Simply wash latex paint brushes in warm soapy water and rinse them in the sink until the water runs clear. Dry them with a paper towel and store with bristles facing up. If you have used oil paint, you will need to clean your brushes with paint thinner and a rag (wear gloves!) and then run them under water to rinse. Follow the instructions on the paint can for best and safest results. Pat the brushes dry with paper towels and store with bristles upright.

Check with your local sanitation or environmental department to understand local paint disposal rules—and follow them!

OUT OF ORDER!

If you are painting everything in a room, do it in order. Start with the ceiling first, then walls, doors, and trim. If you are painting the floor, do that last and don't paint yourself into a corner!

TROUBLE IN PARADISE

Even the pros can run into painting predicaments. Here are some savvy solutions for common problems:

AIR BUBBLES: This usually happens when oil-based gloss paint is applied in bright sunlight or on water-based undercoats. The paint should be removed, the area primed, and then painted out of the direct sun. (Pull the shade but keep the window open!)

BLISTERS: This can be caused by moisture when exposed to the sun. Scrape off the blister, sand it down, and repaint.

BRUSH BRISTLE IN YOUR PAINT: I hate it when this happens! Which is why it's a good idea to invest in high quality brushes. Cheaper brushes have a tendency to shed. But even the best brushes release a little bristle once in a while. If that happens, don't try to pick it out of the wet paint with your fingers. Very gently pick up the bristle with the very edge of the brush and then remove it from the brush with your fingers.

CHIPPING: This is often caused by the topcoat not having a sufficient key. It usually happens when painting on top of an unprimed gloss finish. The only way to prevent this is to prime the gloss surface first or sand the gloss surface down with fine sandpaper and repaint.

COLOR NOT ALL THE SAME SHADE: You may not have stirred the paint properly. Paint should be stirred thoroughly from the bottom before use.

CRACKLING: This happens when old oil paint has hardened and is unable to expand and contract with changing weather conditions. Small crackling can be sanded down, primed, and repainted. Severe crackling on a piece of furniture should be stripped back to bare wood, primed, and repainted.

MILDEW: Remove mildew with a mixture of bleach and water (2 parts water to 1 part bleach) and a sponge. Mildew on walls appears because of moisture in the area. Identify and fix the moisture problem before painting.

RUNNY PAINT: Slow down! Applying paint too heavily normally causes runs. Don't overload your brush with paint. And if runs and drips do happen, brush them out before the paint sets.

Get Plastered

If you live in a home built before World War II (or pre-1950), the chances are very good that your walls are made from plaster over lath, which are strips of wood or metal that provide a means of holding plaster in place. Creating a plaster wall is a pretty labor-intensive job, which is one reason why it's not done anymore. It's just much too expensive. But for those of you who live in older homes, getting to know your plaster walls will help you solve minor plaster problems when they happen.

Lathing strips were first covered with a coarse layer of plaster called a scratch coat. The wet plaster squeezed through the gaps in the lath, locking it to the walls and ceiling. If you have ever seen a hole in a plaster wall, you know what I'm talking about. It looks like cake icing that's dried in between the strips of wood. After the scratch coat dried, a second brown coat was applied to make the surfaces rough but flat. When this layer was dry, the final coat, called a skim coat, was carefully placed on the wall in a thin layer.

Consider yourself lucky to have plaster walls. They are historical and are evidence of great craftspeople of the past. It took a tremendous amount of skill to create a smooth, even plaster wall.

Today, you will often see a skim coat of plaster spread smoothly on top of drywall to replicate a plaster look. It can also be spread on top of brick or stone. It takes years of training and practice to become good at plastering and producing a fine skim coat. But minor repairs are completely doable, and the materials needed are inexpensive and common. It's important to know a few quick plaster fixes, because if you want to paint plaster walls, cracks and holes must be filled and sanded first.

If your plaster problems are major, however, you must call in professional help. For example, if a plaster ceiling looks like it's falling down, it just might be. So use caution and hire a pro to demolish it and replace it with drywall. Furthermore, if there are major cracks in plaster walls, the building may have severe settling problems or water damage. All houses settle, but big cracks may indicate a serious structural problem.

DEFINING MOMENT

BROWN COAT: This is the second, rough coat of plaster.

CORNER BEAD: This wire mesh with a rigid metal spine is used on outside corners.

JOINT COMPOUND: This is a plasterlike substance used to fill seams and irregularities in drywall or plaster.

LATH: Lath strips, which can be made from wood or metal, provide a means of holding plaster in place.

SCRATCH COAT: This is the first coat of plaster set over lath.

SKIM COAT: This is the final plaster coat. It creates a smooth, flat finish.

BARBARA'S BEST-KEPT
SECRET

Plaster dries fast so work
quickly. If the plaster gets too
thick, add a little water as
needed.

Patchwork
Patch a Small Crack in Plaster
Time: 30 minutes, plus drying time

Have you ever taken down a drapery rod or a picture, only to be faced with un-sightly holes left behind by the nails or screws or a crack that was hidden before? That happened to me when I raised the height of my curtains in my living room. But filling the small holes was easy. And when I was done, no one could tell that the rod had been moved from one spot to another.

What You Need

Safety glasses
Mask
Can opener with a curved pointy end
Clean, soft-bristle paintbrush
Fine sandpaper
Joint compound

Plastic cup
Dry plaster of paris
Narrow putty knife
Primer and paint in your wall or
    ceiling color
Paintbrush

How to Get It Done

1. If the crack is in the ceiling, wear safety glasses and a mask.
2. Using the curved end of a can opener, widen the crack so that you can apply patching material in it. No, I'm not kidding. This contractor's secret weapon works better than anything else to open plaster cracks. Be sure to brush away any loose material with a clean, soft-bristle paintbrush.
3. Sand down the edges of the open crack with fine sandpaper.
4. Put joint compound in a plastic cup and mix a little dry plaster of paris powder into the compound. This adds strength to the compound. The amount you use depends on the length and size of the crack, and you may have to add more because joint compound can shrink as it dries. About ¼ cup of joint compound and 1 tablespoon of plaster of paris should be more than enough to fill a small hairline crack.
5. Use a narrow putty knife to spread joint compound along the length of the crack. Push it into the opening and feather it out around the crack. Make it as smooth as possible. If your wall has a stucco effect, mimic the texture by pulling the putty knife straight up to create peaks.

6. Allow the compound to dry. Depending on weather conditions and humidity levels, this could take anywhere from an hour or so to 24 hours

7. Sand the area with fine sandpaper until it is completely smooth. Skip this step if you have a textured effect.

8. Prime the spot. Plaster is absorbent, and priming will help the finish paint coat maintain the same color as the rest of the wall. When the primer is dry, paint the wall.

Patch a Large Crack in Plaster
Time: 40 minutes, plus drying time

Patching a large crack is similar to filling a small crack. Follow instructions for "Patch a Small Crack in Plaster," steps 1 to 4 on the opposite page. Be sure to open the crack wide enough so that all loose plaster is removed and you reach stable plaster. If the crack is very large, a lot of wet joint compound and plaster mix may not want to stick. If that is the case, after step 4, above, complete the process with the following material and steps:

What You Need
Perforated patching tape
Wide putty knife

How to Get It Done
1. Cover the crack with perforated patching tape.
2. Using a putty knife, cover the tape with plaster.
3. Squeeze out any excess plaster by pressing the putty knife along the tape with putty knife. Make sure there are no lumps in the patch.
4. Let the patch dry. Larger patches will take longer to dry than small ones.
5. Sand lightly.
6. Prime and paint.

Step 1. Cover the crack with perforated tape.

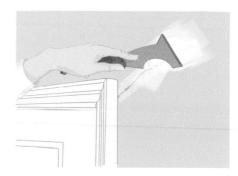

Step 2. Cover the tape with plaster.

Power Patching
Patch Small, Medium, and Large Holes
Time: 40 minutes, plus drying time

Holes in plaster can be fixed in a similar fashion to cracks, but you will need more patching material.

What You Need
- Rubber gloves
- Safety glasses
- Mask
- Can opener with a curved pointy end
- Clean, soft-bristle paintbrush
- Latex bonding liquid
- Paintbrush
- Joint compound
- Plastic cup
- Dry plaster of paris
- Wide putty knife
- Fine sandpaper
- Primer and paint in your wall or ceiling color
- Paintbrush

How to Get It Done
1. Put on rubber gloves to protect your hands. If the hole is in the ceiling, wear safety glasses and a mask.
2. Clean out the hole by scraping with the pointy end of a can opener.
3. Brush out all remaining debris with a soft, clean paintbrush.
4. Paint the edges of the hole about ½ inch outward with latex bonding liquid and a paintbrush.

5. Put some joint compound in a plastic cup and mix it with plaster of paris until it is very stiff. You will have to experiment because there are no exact measurements. You want it as stiff as possible so that it will stay in the hole.
6. Fill the hole using a wide putty knife.
7. Smooth the patching compound around the edges of the hole for the best bond. If the hole is smaller than ¼ inch deep, then one application is sufficient.
8. Large, deep holes will need a second coat of plaster after the first one is dry (you may have to wait 24 hours) because the compound will shrink and may even crack. Don't be alarmed! The second coat will fill in any cracks.
9. Apply latex bonding liquid between the coats.
10. Let the plaster dry.
11. Sand, prime, and paint.

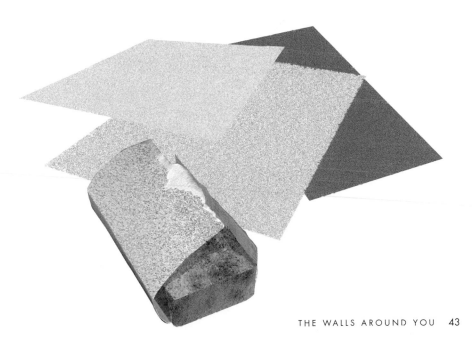

Drywall Details

Most homes built after 1950 have walls constructed from drywall, which is cheaper and faster to install than new plaster walls. Drywall also makes for a very smooth finish that takes paint beautifully. Luckily, drywall is fairly simple to repair when things, uh, *go wrong*. Like the time you were moving a piece of furniture, and (oops) it banged right into the wall and made a dent? No problem. I have fixed a drywall dent after work and still had time to get ready for a date. You can, too!

The downside of drywall is that drywall sheets are very heavy, so I would not recommend installing it yourself. And forget about installing a ceiling on your own. Call in the pros for installation, but save time and money by making repairs yourself. Your walls and wallet will thank you!

DEFINING MOMENT

CORNER BEAD: This is a smaller metal or plastic strip, bent at a 90-degree angle that goes over the corner guard to protect the guard and to create a finished corner. This, along with the guard, is covered with a skim coat of joint compound to create a smooth edge.

CORNER GUARD: This is a metal edge bent at a 90-degree angle to fit over outside corners of walls. It is attached with drywall nails, which go through ready-made holes. It helps to join drywall at corners. It needs to be covered with a corner bead compound to create a smooth, seamless edge.

DRYWALL OR WALLBOARD: These are usually 4- by 8-foot sheets made of gypsum or plaster wrapped in paper that can be nailed to wall studs to form smooth, regular walls.

FURRING STRIP: This is a strip of wood used to give a level surface for attaching wallboard.

POPPED NAIL: This is a Sheetrock nail head that protrudes from the wall.

SHEETROCK: This is simply a brand name for the generic term drywall or wallboard. The three terms are interchangeable.

STUD: A wood or sometimes metal 2×4 or 2×6 used to frame walls and partitions, they are normally placed every 16 inches along a wall and attach to a floor and ceiling track. Keeping that in mind, once you have found the first stud, it is easy to locate the others by measuring.

Pop Problem Solved
Repair Popped Nails
Time: About 20 minutes, plus drying time

Popped nails are very common in new construction because the builder may have
used unseasoned wood for the studs or furring strips behind the drywall. When that
unseasoned wood starts to dry out, it can shrink, causing the nail head to pop out.
It's an easy problem to fix.

What You Need

Hammer

Drywall nail

Nail set

Putty knife

Joint compound

Fine sandpaper

Paint in your wall or ceiling color

Paintbrush

Step 3. Tap the nail just
below the surface.

How to Get It Done

1. Tap the popped nail flush to the wall with a hammer.
2. Place the point of another drywall nail next to the nail you've just hammered.
   Drive it in so the head is overlapping the first nail head.
3. Using a nail set, tap the nail heads into the wall, just below the surface.
4. Use a putty knife to cover the dent made by the countersunk nails with joint
   compound. Be sure to smooth the compound as best you can.
5. When the joint compound is dry (2 to 24 hours, depending on weather conditions), sand it lightly until smooth. Avoid sanding the drywall area that is not
   affected by the nails. The paint may come off and the paper covering might tear.
6. Apply another thin coat of joint compound over the patch.
7. Wait until that dries completely, then sand it again. Again, avoid sanding the
   drywall area that is not affected by the nails.
8. Paint the area with matching color.

Crack the Case
Repair Split Drywall Tape
Time: About 40 minutes, plus drying time

Drywall tape is placed on all the seams where the drywall sheets meet. Sometimes the tape can shrink and split, usually if it's gotten wet and then dried. The shrinking tape will cause the joint compound covering it to crack. If you think a leak behind the wall caused the trouble, identify the origin and get it fixed; otherwise the wall will keep cracking.

What You Need
Utility knife
Putty knife
Joint compound
Paper drywall tape
Rag or sponge
Fine sandpaper
Primer and paint in your wall or ceiling color
Paintbrush

How to Get It Done

1. Using a sharp utility knife, carefully cut out the loose tape around the split. Don't remove tape that is attached, or you may rip the paper coating the drywall.
2. Using a putty knife, apply a thin layer of joint compound, about 4 inches wide and 2 inches above and below the area.
3. Lay a 2-inch wide piece of paper drywall tape into the wet joint compound. Force it into the compound by pulling your putty knife over it.
4. Remove any excess compound that comes out of the sides with a damp rag or sponge.
5. Wait for the compound to dry. This could take up to 24 hours, depending on humidity conditions.
6. Use fine sandpaper to sand down the dried compound. Take care not to raise the fibers of the tape.
7. Apply another layer of compound.
8. Wait until that layer dries completely, then apply another layer of compound.
9. After the final layer of compound has dried, sand it one more time with fine sandpaper.
10. Prime and paint the area with matching wall color.

Dent Mend
Fill in a Dent
Time: 40 minutes, plus drying time

Dents and small holes can't be disguised with a lick of paint. You really have to fill them in if you don't want to look at them. This is especially true if you are planning to repaint your room. All the work and time you put in to give your room a fresh coat of paint will be wasted if holes are not filled in beforehand.

What You Need
Fine sandpaper
Putty knife
Joint compound
Primer and paint in your wall or ceiling color
Paintbrush

How to Get It Done
1. Lightly sand the dent and surrounding wall with fine sandpaper. Aggressive sanding will scratch the paper on the drywall.
2. Use your putty knife to fill the dent with joint compound.
3. When the compound is dry, sand the area down until it is smooth and flush with the wall.
4. Apply another thin layer of compound on top of the patch and let that dry thoroughly.
5. When the final coating of compound is dry, smooth the surface with fine sandpaper.
6. Prime and paint the area with matching wall color.

Compound the Problem
Patch Small to Medium Holes in Drywall
Time: 60 to 90 minutes, plus drying time

Small- and medium-size holes (2 inches or smaller) can be filled with joint compound and covered with fiberglass tape. I had to use this technique when a friend accidentally opened a door a bit too forcefully and the glass knob created a gash in the wall.

What You Need
- Putty knife
- Joint compound
- Fiberglass tape
- Fine sandpaper
- Primer and paint in your wall or ceiling color
- Paintbrush

How to Get It Done
1. Using a putty knife, fill the hole with joint compound and stretch fiberglass tape across the hole.
2. Apply two or three coats of joint compound on top of the tape. Allow drying time between each layer and sand between coats.
3. Prime and paint when the final layer is dry and sanded.

Patch Large Holes
Time: About 90 minutes, plus drying time

Large holes need to be patched with drywall. This takes a bit more skill than filling a dent or small hole, but it's worth the effort. Don't be afraid—you won't ruin your wall! Just take it slow.

What You Need

Utility knife or keyhole saw
1- by 3-inch piece pine wood for backer board
Crosscut saw
1¼-inch drywall screws
Power drill with screwdriver bits
Drywall scrap for patching hole
Self-sticking fiberglass tape
Putty knife
Joint compound
Fine sandpaper
Primer and paint in your wall or ceiling color
Paintbrush

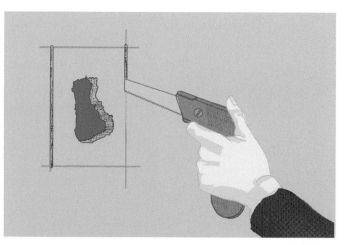

Step 1. Cut a square larger than the hole.

How to Get It Done

1. Using a utility knife or keyhole saw, cut a square area larger than the hole.
2. Using a piece of scrap 1- by 3-inch pine wood, cut two backer boards with a crosscut saw 2 to 3 inches wider than the hole.
3. Place the first backer board inside the hole and place it at the top edge of the opening. Secure it with 1¼-inch drywall screws and follow the manufacturer's instructions for using your electric drill as a screwdriver. Hold the board in place as you work. Tighten until the screw heads are below the surface.
4. Place the second backer board inside lower edge of the opening. Repeat step 3 to secure it.
5. Cut a scrap piece of drywall with the utility knife to fit snug in the opening. Score the drywall with a utility knife on one side and then break each side off until you have the desired size.
6. Screw the drywall patch to the backer boards and tighten until the screw heads are below the surface.
7. Apply strips of self-sticking fiberglass tape over all four seams.
8. Using your putty knife, cover the tape with a thin coat of joint compound. When the joint compound is dry, sand lightly with fine sandpaper.
9. Apply two more coats of joint compound, letting it dry and feathering and sanding each coat.
10. Prime and paint the drywall patch.

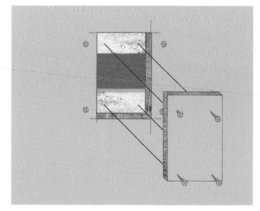

Step 6. Screw the patch to the backer board.

Step 8. Cover the tape with a thin coat of joint compound.

BARBARA'S BEST-KEPT SECRET

To best determine the placement of large artwork or mirrors, trace the frame onto a big piece of construction paper first. Put the paper on the wall and play around with the placement until you find the right spot. Mark one or two corners with a pencil and then just line your frame up to get the same position.

Hanging a row of mirrors is an easy way to create the illusion of light and space.

Mirrors, Mirrors, on the Wall
Hang Pictures and Mirrors
Time: 15 to 20 minutes per picture or mirror

Photographs and artwork make a space come alive and tell visitors a story about you and your life. Family photos are too precious to tuck away in boxes. Display them so you can enjoy them everyday. I don't think my day would be very happy if pictures of my parents, my sister, and especially my son didn't surround me!

Mirrors are another way to brighten up a room—literally. Mirrors reflect light and can help make long hallways or dark rooms beam. I placed a collection of mirrors down my hallway, and it doubled the amount of light in the space.

When hanging groups of pictures or mirrors, think about size, shape, and frame and mat color. Different style frames can be unified through color. The unifying theme of my "hall of mirrors" is color: All of them are white.

What You Need

Tape measure
Pencil
Adhesive tape

Picture hook and nail
Hammer
Level

How to Get It Done

1. Determine where you want to put your pictures or mirrors. A basic guideline to follow is to center the picture approximately 66 to 68 inches above the floor or 12 to 16 inches centered above a piece of furniture. Use a tape measure to measure correctly. No matter what your ceiling height, you want pictures to be at eye level.
2. Secure the picture hook by placing a small piece of adhesive tape on the wall below the pencil mark. This will help prevent the drywall or plaster from cracking. Now, place the nail through the picture hook and hammer it into the wall. The nail should be at a 45 degree angle to the wall.
3. Hang a picture by the wire on the back of the frame. Make any necessary adjustments so that the picture is level, using a level to check for sure.

This simple row of mirrors in my hallway is elegant and very modern.

Wild for Wallpaper

Wallpaper has many great uses in different areas. But there's a good chance that you will get bored with your paper choice before it wears out. While wallpaper isn't exactly permanent, it's also not that easy to remove. It takes time and patience and can be a very messy job.

Wallpaper is also very challenging to install. Matching patterns and getting paper on straight can be nerve-racking. Many happy couples have called it quits after trying to infuse a room with country charm by hanging floor-to-ceiling buffalo plaid paper, only to wind up feeling all boxed in.

If you do have your heart set on paper, though, think about starting out small by hanging a border or perhaps papering an alcove, niche, or accent wall. Small doses of pattern go a long way, and it may be all you need to create the mood you're after.

Unless you are a very experienced home decorator, I think it would be a frustrating project for you to install your own wallpaper. I recommend hiring professional help when installing large areas of wallpaper. This is particularly important if you have chosen a stripe or plaid pattern, a textured paper, or a mural scene, which require precise matching skills.

DEFINING MOMENT

BOOKING: This is the technique of wetting and then folding the wet side of the paper in on itself to prepare it for hanging.

SINGLE ROLL: 25 feet of wallpaper on one continuous roll. Keep in mind that most wallpaper is priced per single roll—but sold in double rolls.

DOUBLE ROLL: Many commercial papers are sold on double rolls of 50 feet of wallpaper, but high end or handmade papers are more often sold as single rolls.

REPEAT: This is the motif on a roll of paper that is repeated over and over to create an overall pattern.

SCORING TOOL, OR TIGER: A plastic disc or puck-shaped tool with sharp, zigzag teeth that you run across the wallpaper. This perforates the paper so that you can spray or sponge on water or a formula of fabric softener and water to soften the paste and enable you to peel the paper off the wall.

SEAM ROLLER: This is a flat rubber roller that helps remove bubbles and flattens paper at seams.

STEAMER: This is a rectangular, flat iron or sorts, generally electric, that you run across the papered wall. The heat and moist steam softens the paste and makes tearing off paper easier. You can rent steamers for $50 to $100 a day, approximately.

WALLPAPER PASTE OR GLUE: The glue that is used to stick paper to the wall. Most often available in premixed formulas.

If you're willing and able to pay for professional application, go to the store prepared. This means bringing along fabric swatches and paint chips from the room to be papered. (This is a perfect use for your inspiration board. Bring it along with you.) Shopping for patterns can be overwhelming because there are literally thousands of wallpaper patterns and hundreds of wallpaper sample books available to peruse. Give yourself a break and limit yourself to three or four books at a time. Focus on a particular style so that you can eliminate the need to look at certain categories. For example, if you are going for modern, you can automatically skip floral, fruits, and representational prints (think hearts, little houses, or French toile). Talk to the people in the paper department at the store and ask for help in steering you toward those manufacturers who can best fill your needs.

If you already have paper in your home and it needs repair, you can fix it without having to reinstall or remove it (unless you want to). Common paper problems are easy to solve.

Blister Bliss
Fix Blisters and Bubbles
Time: About 20 minutes

Little blisters in wallpaper are unattractive, but they can be repaired in a matter of minutes. It's a good idea to attend to them, too, so they don't grow larger and create a more severe problem (and a more time-consuming repair job).

What You Need
Utility knife

How to Get It Done
1. Cut a small X in the middle of the bubble with a utility knife.
2. Follow the directions and use the materials on page 56 for fixing torn wallpaper.

A-Peeling Fix
Repair Peeling or Torn Wallpaper
Time: About 20 minutes

Paper can peel from the top of the wall if the paper has gotten damp and then dried too fast or if the weather has gone from humid to dry very quickly. The glue on older wallpaper can simply get old and dry out and then cause it to peel. A tear can happen for any number of reasons, most having to do with human intervention.

What You Need

Sponge
Wallpaper paste
Small paintbrush
Squeegee, seam roller, or plastic putty knife

How to Get It Done

1. Dampen a sponge.
2. Gently pull the torn or separated paper away from the wall to expose the underside of the paper.
3. Moisten the underside of the paper with the sponge.
4. Brush a thin, even coat of wallpaper paste on the paper with a small paintbrush.
5. Smooth the paper against the wall using a squeegee, seam roller, or plastic putty knife. (A plastic putty knife is less likely to damage the paper than a metal knife.)
6. As a precaution, let the repair dry before hanging any pictures or moving furniture against the repaired wall.

Seamless Solution
Stop Separating Seams
Time: About 30 minutes

Separating seams, like blisters, can become worse if not addressed right away.

What You Need
Sponge
Wallpaper paste
Plastic putty knife
Seam roller

How to Get It Done
1. Moisten the area where the paper has separated with a damp sponge.
2. *Gently* pull the loose paper away from the wall, along the separated seams.
3. Apply wallpaper paste to the underside of the paper.
4. Using a plastic putty knife, smooth the paper from the outside toward the seam on either side, placing gentle pressure on the paper to pull each side closer to the center.
5. Finish by rolling the newly pasted seam flat with a seam roller.

Match and Patch
Patch a Tear
Time: About 40 minutes, including waiting time

If your wallpaper has torn and the damaged piece cannot be salvaged or put back into place, you will have to "match and patch" with a spare piece of paper. You may be saying to yourself that there's no way you can make an invisible patch, but it's not as difficult as it sounds. It's all in the cutting.

What You Need
Pencil
Ruler
Extra wallpaper for patching
Painter's tape
Utility knife
Sponge
Putty knife
Paintbrush
Wallpaper paste
Seam roller

Step 3. Tape the wallpaper patch over the damaged area.

Step 5. Cut the 3-inch square on the patch.

How to Get It Done

1. Using a pencil and a ruler, draw a 3-inch square around the torn or missing piece. Extend the lines of each corner 6 inches.
2. Cut a piece of the extra wallpaper in a square that is 6 inches larger than the square you drew on your wall.
3. Tape the piece over the damaged area using painter's tape. (Masking tape can potentially damage the wallpaper surface further.) Be sure to match the patterns!
4. Using the extended lines as a guide, use your pencil and ruler to draw the same square on the paper as you did on the wall.
5. Using a utility knife and your ruler as a straightedge and with gentle pressure, cut along the lines through both the patch and the paper on the wall.
6. Remove the top square and put it aside. Using a damp sponge, wet the wall area where you scored. Wait 10 to 20 minutes, then gently remove the square from the wall.
7. Use a paintbrush to apply wallpaper paste to the back of the patch you cut. Apply it to the wall using a clean damp sponge and smooth out all four sides with a seam roller.

Step 6. After wetting the damaged area, use a putty knife to remove the square of old wallpaper.

Removing Wallpaper

At this point, you may be tired of repairing wallpaper problems and want to simply get rid of the stuff. I can't say I blame you! There are two methods for removing wallpaper. Neither is foolproof, and both require a time commitment. You can rent a steamer from an equipment rental center or home improvement store and steam it off. Or you can buy a scoring tool and remove it that way. If you have a lot of wallpaper to remove, renting a steamer is the way to go. It will be a lot faster than scoring, wiping down, and peeling by hand, especially if you need to remove more than one layer of wallpaper. But it's still not a fast fix. Reserve a day for this project.

Generally you do not have to score wallpaper if you are planning on using a steamer. I do suggest covering your floor with a canvas (not plastic) drop cloth to catch the messy paper as it peels off. I also recommend asking a friend or relative to help you. One of you can steam while the other peels off the loosened paper.

Most steamers operate in a similar fashion, but please follow the manufacturer's instructions for yours. Ask the rental agent for a demonstration. Because they want their items returned in good order, they will be more than happy to give you a lesson. Finally, remember that the steamer is hot, so use work gloves when operating and go slowly, especially in the beginning, as you get a feel for how yours works.

The Great Rip-Off
Remove Wallpaper
Time: 4 to 10 hours, depending on the size of your room

If you have a small area to deal with, such as a bathroom or one wall in a room, it may not be worth the expense to rent a steamer. Scoring, dampening, and peeling may work just as well in this instance.

What You Need

Scoring tool

Canvas drop cloth

Bucket or paint tray

Fabric softener

Paint roller with a thick nap or large
 bone-shaped sponge

Rubber gloves

Safety glasses

Plastic putty knife

Sponge

How to Get It Done

1. Score the surface of the wallpaper with a scoring tool by running it all over the surface in a circular motion. The scoring tool will come with instructions. Read and follow them. It's worth investing in a scoring tool because they cost less than $10 and are made specifically for wallpaper removal. You may be tempted to score the wall with a utility knife, but it's very hard to control the sharp edge of the knife, and you may end up cutting through the paper and into the wall.
2. Cover the floor with a canvas drop cloth. Do not use a plastic drop cloth.
3. Fill a bucket or paint tray with a solution of 1 part water and 1 part fabric softener. There is no reason to pay extra money for wallpaper removal gels or liquids. Wallpaper paste is water-soluble and normally does not need expensive chemicals to soften it.
4. Using a paint roller or a sponge, apply the water and softener mixture very liberally to the wall. Wear rubber gloves and safety glasses because the mixture can spatter.
5. Allow the mixture to soak into the wallpaper for about 30 minutes.
6. Starting at the bottom of the wall or at a seam, gently pull away the old paper.
7. Use a plastic putty knife to remove any remaining glue and paper from the wall.
8. Once the paper and glue are completely removed, wipe down the wall with water and a clean sponge.

Preparation Is Everything
Prepare a Wall for Painting or New Wallpaper
Time: 4 to 10 hours, depending on the size of your room and the condition of its walls

Once you have your wallpaper off, you will want to repaint the room (or maybe you want to have new paper applied). The walls need to repaired and prepared before proceeding with paint or new paper.

What You Need
Drop cloth
Painter's tape
Paint tray
Paint roller
Paintbrush
Stain-blocking primer
Interior wall paint in desired color

How to Get It Done
1. If the surface of the wall behind the wallpaper is damaged, you will need to repair it before painting or applying new wallpaper. See the instructions and material lists on pages 40 to 51 in this chapter for repairing drywall or plaster problems.
2. Prepare the room for painting by covering the floor and furnishings with a drop cloth and taping off surfaces you don't want painted with painter's tape. Using a paint tray and a paint roller and paintbrushes, paint on a fresh coat of stain-blocking primer before repainting or papering the wall.
3. If you are planning on repapering the wall, paint the wall a color that closely matches the dominant color in your wallpaper pattern. With this step, if the seams do separate slightly (but don't come away from the wall), the seam will not show as much as it would if the wall was a contrasting color.

A Covert Operation
Paint over Wallpaper
Time: About 8 hours, depending on the size of the room and the condition of its walls

If you want to paint a room that has been papered, it's better to remove the wallpaper first, as described on page 61. But if you simply don't have the time to remove the paper and paint the room, too, painting over paper can be a viable alternative. Just know that removing the wallpaper later will be all the more difficult because of the paint. If you want to get rid of dated or yellowing paper in a kitchen or bath, painting over it can be a time-saving solution.

What You Need

Drop cloth	Paint tray and roller
Painter's tape	Paintbrush
Water-based white glue	Fine sandpaper
Seam roller	Interior wall paint
Stain-blocking primer	

How to Get It Done

1. Prepare the room for painting by covering the floor and furnishings with a drop cloth and taping off surfaces you don't want painted with painter's tape.
2. Because you can only paint over paper that is securely pasted to the wall, inspect the paper and glue down loose edges. Refer to the instructions on page 58 for repairing wallpaper tears, peeling paper, or bubbles. Seal loose seams with water-based white glue and press the seams down securely with a seam roller.
3. Let all repairs dry before painting.
4. Apply one coat of stain-blocking primer from a paint tray with a roller and brush. Consider tinting the primer to match the paint you plan to use in the room. Let it dry. If you can still see the wallpaper pattern through the primer, apply another coat.
5. If the wallpaper seams are visible after two coats of primer, lightly file the seams smooth with fine sandpaper.
6. Apply the paint. Let it dry. Depending on the color, you may have to apply a second coat. (Dark colors may need more than one coat to appear opaque.)

BARBARA'S BEST-KEPT SECRET

Periodically wipe the paint buildup off the stencil using a clean damp sponge. Don't let the paint dry completely on the stencil.

Fake It
Paint a Pattern
Time: 2 to 3 hours, depending on how complicated the stencil is

Instead of driving yourself crazy putting up wallpaper, consider stenciling your wall in a repeating pattern that looks like wallpaper. You really can achieve a truly professional custom wallpaper look using wall stencils. In fact, this technique is also a lot less expensive than wallpapering. And if you don't like it or you get bored with it, it's a snap to get rid of: Simply paint right over it and start again. I liked the headboard so much I did a tone-on-tone pattern on my bedroom's fireplace wall. Your wall stencil will come with instructions, but here are general guidelines.

What You Need
Latex background paint

Latex glaze

Painter's tape

Pencil

Tape measure

Wall stencil

Repositional spray adhesive

Cardboard

Paint tray

Latex paint for stencil

High-density foam stencil roller

Paper towels

Practice board

Sponge

How to Get It Done
1. If you want the background of your stencil to be different than your wall color, paint it. My background was faux finished using a mixture of 50 percent glaze and 50 percent paint. I sponged it on over the existing wall color. If you are painting only the center of the wall, as I did, be sure to mark off the sides with painter's tape to create a straightedge.

2. Once the background color was dry, I marked a level line where I wanted my stencil, using a pencil and tape measure. If you're doing the entire height of the wall, as I did, start the stencil at the top center of the area you are stenciling.

3. Lightly spray the back of the stencil with repositionable spray stencil adhesive. This adhesive, available at any craft or art supply store, is low tack and so allows you to peel off the stencil and reposition it without leaving any sticky adhesive on the wall. You can use the stencil four or five times before you have to re-spray. If it seems too tacky, stick it to a piece of cardboard once or twice to remove excess tack.

Before: My bedroom was pretty blah before I made it over.

4. Line up two small guides cut in the stencil with the level horizontal line. Don't use the edge of the stencil as a guide. Press the stencil to the surface and mark a pencil or pin dot in the top of each of the guide holes.

5. Pour your paint into a paint tray. Paint over the stencil with the high-density foam stencil roller. This is the most important piece of equipment in this project! It will allow the paint to go on smoothly and evenly. It doesn't soak up too much paint, so it will also discourage dripping. However, be sure to blot almost all the paint on a paper towel before you put it on the wall. If you are feeling unsure, use the practice board that is included with the stencil to master the technique first.

6. When you're done with the first section, carefully peel off the stencil to the repeat position by lining up the two guide holes with the pin dots you made. Position the stencil, mark the guide holes for the next spot, and paint. Continue this way until the wall or section of the wall is complete.

After: My gorgeous new "headboard" looks like expensive brocade wallpaper, but it's just paint.

OPPOSITE: Stenciling is really easy, but the result is professional and artistic.

Paneling Particulars

When I hear the word "paneling," I immediately think about basement walls or family rooms covered in dark knotty pine. Wood paneling like that was very popular in the 1970s and consequently, you may live in a home from that era and have a paneled room . . . or two. Some wood paneling can be very beautiful and rich looking. For example, raised panel wainscoting is a very traditional material perfect for a den or library. And crisp white bead board panels can add texture and detail to a room where none exists. New paneling products, such as easily installed sheets of beaded plywood, have come a long way since the '70s, making a potentially expensive proposition of adding architectural detail to a room relatively inexpensive.

But if you do have Brady Bunch–era paneling in a room and you don't like it, there are alternatives to taking it down and dealing with what might be underneath. It's easy to make minor repairs to run-down wood walls, and a coat of paint can give old panels a completely modern look.

DEFINING MOMENT

BEAD BOARD: These are sheets of 4- by 8-foot wood or sometimes plastic that has grooves cut into it at regular intervals, creating the look of traditional tongue and groove paneling. Bead board paneling is thinner, lighter, and much easier to install than tongue and groove. It can also be used to cover a ceiling.

PANELING: These sheets of wood or plastic made to look like wood are meant to cover full walls of a room. The grooves cut in the paneling are often at irregular intervals and much wider than those cut in bead board paneling. They may be attached directly to the studs in an older house.

RAISED PANELING: These boards have bevels on all four sides of one face so that it is thicker in the center than at its perimeter.

TONGUE AND GROOVE: These boards or planks have been finished so that there is a groove on one side of the board and a corresponding tongue on the other edge. When two pieces are placed together, the tongue of one will fit into the groove of another, forming a natural joint between the two boards. They're often used in wall siding.

WAINSCOT: This is a wooden lining of walls often covering the lower part only of the wall. Wainscot is often done in bead board or raised panels.

Panel on the Loose
Secure Loose Paneling
Time: About 20 minutes

Sometimes paneling can buckle or start to come away from the wall, especially in paneled basements, where moisture is an annoying fact of life. The easiest way to fix a loose board is by nailing it into place. You can pry the whole sheet off and reapply construction adhesive and then put it back into place. But this may involve removing floor and ceiling molding and trim. Because the nail fix is strong, fast, and easy, I recommend it over the pry-and-glue method.

What You Need
Hammer
2-inch nails
Nail set
Paint or wax touch-up stain sticks to match paneling

How to Get It Done
1. Remove any loose nails from the loose paneling using a hammer.
2. Using the nail holes in the grooves as a guide, use fresh 2-inch nails to nail the paneling to the wall.
3. If there are no nail holes to guide you, be sure to nail in the groove—not in the panel itself. The nails will be less visible in the grooves.
4. Stop nailing when the head is about to go into the groove space. Drive in the nail the rest of the way using a nail set.
5. Finally, touch up the nail head, if necessary, using the stain stick.

From Brown to Beautiful
Paint a Paneled Wall
Time: 12 hours, including drying time

A fresh coat of light, bright semigloss, satin, or eggshell finish paint will instantly give old paneling a modern, clean look.

What You Need
    Denatured alcohol
    Sponges
    Mask
    Safety glasses
    Rubber gloves
    Fine sandpaper
    Putty knife
    Joint compound
    Stain-blocking primer
    Paint tray
    Paintbrushes
    Roller
    Wall paint in a semigloss, satin, or eggshell finish

How to Get It Done
1. Wash the walls with denatured alcohol on a sponge. This will get rid of grease and grime that will hinder painting. It will also dull any sheen the paneling may have. Denatured alcohol emits fumes, so be sure your room is well ventilated and wear a mask and safety glasses. Wear rubber gloves to protect your hands.
2. Once the walls are dry, sand down any bumps and rough spots with fine sandpaper.
3. Using your putty knife, fill any knotholes or other holes with joint compound. Once it is dry, sand spots smooth.

4. Wipe the spots with a damp sponge to remove any dust.

5. When dry, prime with stain-blocking primer sealer. It gives a smooth surface nap so the paint will hold. If you don't use stain-blocking primer, the resins in knots and graining will allow them to show through. Plus, the primer sealer eliminates the need to "de-gloss" the wood with chemicals.

6. Once the primer is completely dry (in humid conditions, you may want to wait overnight), roll on your first coat of paint from a paint tray and cut in with a paintbrush.

7. Depending on the color you choose, it may be necessary to give the paneling a second (and even a third) coat of paint. Wait until each coat is completely dry before judging whether you need another. If you do, paint the paneling again, and wait for it to dry.

Your walls are in order—you've filled cracks, plastered holes, and painted your rooms in the colors that make you happy. Next stop: floors.

Chapter 3
Floor Show

There are so many options in flooring today; it's possible to achieve just about any kind of look from rustic to modern and everything in between. *Think about it:* Great rooms go country with wide plank wood floors rescued from a barn, and tradition is maintained in a den or living room with the help of classic tongue and groove oak flooring. Bamboo flooring brings Asian flair to a family room. Pop the cork (flooring, that is) in kitchens or anyplace comfort underfoot is desired. Ceramic, clay, or stone tile evokes a Mediterranean or tropical mood in a dining area or sunroom. Colorful carpet tiles let your imagination run rampant. And that's just the beginning. All of these ideas can be turned upside down and inside out to suit you. In short, it's a floor show, and you're the star!

Choosing the right material for your floors is essential because the floor sets a room's tone. It's part of the canvas that you will fill with furnishings, rugs, accessories, and your family and friends. This means a floor needs to suit both your style *and* your lifestyle. When replacing floor coverings, always keep in mind how the space will be used, how much traffic it will get, and how much maintenance time you can devote to whatever material you put down, because some floors are simply more durable than others and need less upkeep. Wall-to-wall carpeting, for example, may not be practical in an entryway or mudroom. Wood flooring is tough to care for in a bathroom because of the dampness factor.

SAFETY NOTES

Remember to always follow the manufacturer's instructions when using any product or tool, even if you've used it in the past. Manufacturers take a lot of time to write user-friendly instructions, and they know better than anyone about how to use their particular materials and tools.

Also remember when embarking on any floor or stair project to work in any area that has been cleared of debris, or any breakable or movable objects. In the case of stairs, make sure you are working in a secure and stable area. Never place or try to balance a ladder on stairs.

Even if you are working in a small area, protect what's around you. When working with paints or solvents of any kind, make sure the room is well ventilated. Wear a mask and safety glasses for protection against fumes and dust. Please dispose of solvents in a way that complies with local environmental rules.

Some flooring projects are do-it-yourself easy. However, installing broadloom carpeting, new wood floors, or heavy pieces of stone in large areas is best left to the pros. Specialized tools are needed for such projects, along with the skills to use them. But the result is always worth it: A high-quality floor of any kind, professionally installed, should last a very long time. So if you *are* thinking about new flooring, be assured that, chosen wisely, it's a good investment that adds value to your home. Hardwood flooring and stone or ceramic tiles, for example, are considered desirable upgrades by real estate pros.

Here's more good news: If you don't have new flooring in your future, don't worry. You can take control of the floors that you already have. Breathe new life into wooden floors by repairing minor scratches and dents or by painting over world-weary floorboards. Peel-and-stick vinyl tile gives a mudroom, laundry or utility room, or even a kitchen a fresh update in just an afternoon. I'll even show you how to tile a bathroom floor with 12- by 12-inch sheets of mosaic tile using just a few basic tiling skills. It's an impressive *and* affordable way to turn your bathroom into a spa-like retreat.

So let's start getting underfoot!

Wood Is Good

I love the warmth and natural beauty of wood. I have wood floors throughout my house, including painted wood floors in the kitchen. Wood is so versatile: It looks right in most settings and works with every style, be it traditional, contemporary, country, or urban. When properly cared for, wood can last for a very long time: Two-hundred-year-old houses regularly have their original flooring in place. Hardwood flooring such as oak and maple can be sanded down and refinished many times. Softwood, like pine, is easily dented and dinged, lending a more rustic look to a room. All woods can be painted, stained and waxed, or coated with polyurethane for a hard finish that can hold up well, even in a kitchen.

When buying a wood floor, keep in mind how it will be delivered. Wood floors come as either prefinished or unfinished. An unfinished floor has to be sanded, stained, and coated in your house, which can be messy and inconvenient. Prefinished floors are a bit more expensive, but they are ready to walk on as soon as they are laid.

Regardless of the type of wood flooring you choose, it should have only 7 to 10 percent moisture content; ask about it before you buy. A floor that has too much moisture will dry differently than one with lower moisture content. Such floors will shift and separate more than floors that have been dried properly before installation.

If you already live in a home with hardwood flooring throughout, consider yourself lucky—and take good care of them.

DEFINING MOMENT

HARDWOOD. Hardwoods come from deciduous trees (those that loose their leaves in the fall). Hardwood is denser and heavier than softwood, which makes it strong and sturdy enough for flooring and fine furniture. Hardwood typically used in flooring includes red and white oak, maple, mahogany, poplar, birch, and walnut. Many hardwoods are very expensive to use as flooring, such as mahogany and walnut. Oak and maple are more readily available and therefore more affordable.

PLAIN SAWING: Wood is brought to mills in the form of long logs. First, the bark is removed from the log and then it is rough-cut to prepare it for milling. One way wood is cut is by plain sawing it, which simply means planks are cut straight from one end of the log to the other. Wood shrinks as it dries, and plain-cut wood has a tendency to warp when dry, making it less desirable for flooring.

QUARTER-SAWN: This is wood that's cut in quarters diagonally so that each of the four pieces is at a 90-degree angle. Planks are then cut from the quarter-sawn pieces. The angle cut makes this lumber much more stable and warp-resistant than plain-cut wood,

making it desirable for flooring. When buying wood flooring, ask the dealer if it's quarter-sawn.

RECLAIMED WOOD: This is wood that has been rescued from barns and other old buildings. It is generally taken to a mill and replaned for use as flooring and other applications. Using reclaimed wood is recycling at its best. The best way to find reclaimed wood suppliers is by searching the Internet for reclaimed wood flooring. It's a specialty product, so most flooring retailers will not carry it.

SOFTWOOD: Softwoods are commonly used in the construction side of building and less often for flooring. Softwoods come from the fir family of evergreens, which includes pine. Pine is sometimes used for flooring, but it dents easily and is less versatile than hardwood flooring. Because softwoods are less expensive, they are often used for moldings, cabinets, and trim. Some common softwood varieties are pine, Douglas fir, cedar, hemlock, and redwood. Cedar, pine, and redwood are often used for outdoor decks, cedar and redwood because of their natural ability to resist changes in weather. Pressure-treated pine is commonly used

because it's inexpensive. For many years, pine was treated with a combination of chemicals that included arsenic, but that is no longer available. In 2002 the U.S. Environmental Protection Agency (EPA) announced a voluntary decision by the lumber industry to stop treating consumer lumber products with arsenic and other harmful chemicals. Less harmful alternative wood preservatives are now being used in pressure-treated lumber.

TONGUE AND GROOVE: These are boards or planks of wood that are cut so that there is a groove on one side of the board and a lip or tongue on the other, making it possible to tightly lock one plank of wood to another. Most wood flooring is tongue and groove, although some reclaimed wood planking used for flooring is cut straight on the sides and is simply butted up, one against the other, and nailed into place.

WOOD LAMINATE: Wood laminates are made from several layers of wood that are bound together with glue and pressure and topped with a thin veneer of hardwood. The layers are placed so the grain direction alternates, for strength, durability, and stability.

De-Scratch

Fix a Scratch

Time: About 30 minutes, plus drying time

I love rearranging my furniture, and even though I put slides on the bottom of all my large and heavy pieces, scratches are an inevitable part of redoing a room. Plus, my son, Zachary, and I love to play games on the floor, and well, sometimes accidents just have a way of happening. No big deal. Having fun with Zach is more important to me than any floor. In any case, most scratch accidents can be easily fixed, even if they have removed the stain from the wood. You can also use this technique for matching stains on furniture.

What You Need

Wood stain that matches the color of your floor
Paint stick for mixing
Fine sandpaper
Paint thinner
Muffin tin (do not reuse for food)
Teaspoon (do not reuse for food)
Artist's brushes
Varnish or polyurethane that matches the finish of your floor
Clean rags
Paper towels

How to Get It Done

1. Select a wood stain appropriate for your floor that most closely resembles its color. Follow the directions on the can for preparation, which usually includes stirring gently from the bottom up with a paint stick.
2. Find an inconspicuous spot on your floor where you can perform a color-matching test, such as under a rug or in a closet. Using fine sandpaper, sand down four small areas to reveal the level of scratch you are planning on restoring.
3. Mix the stain with paint thinner in separate cups of an old muffin tin in the following ratios: straight out of the can, 4 to 1, 2 to 1, and 1 to 1. Use an old teaspoon to measure out the quantities. One teaspoon equals one part. So, for

OPPOSITE: My wood floors are beautiful and sturdy, but sometimes they get scratched.

BARBARA'S BEST-KEPT SECRET

This is a quick fix for surface scratches that takes less than 15 seconds per scratch.

Rubbing a bit of clear lip balm or petroleum jelly into surface scratches will make them disappear. This simple technique can also be used on surface scratches on marble and granite, although it's not as long lasting. Try it. You'll be amazed!

If a hairline scratch is deeper than the finish, special stain colored "magic markers" will cover and seal the scratch. After the marker dries (it only takes a few seconds) a little lip balm on top will create a seal.

example, the 4 to 1 ratio would be 4 teaspoons of paint thinner to 1 teaspoon of stain. Stir each mixture with the spoon.

4. Apply a small amount of each mixture to a test spot using an artist's brush.
5. When all four spots are dry, apply varnish or polyurethane (whichever is used on your floor to protect it) to the test spots. This will darken them. When the finish has completely dried, you will be able to see which test matches the floor best.
6. Apply the matching mixture to the real scratch using an artist's brush. Hold the brush as close to its neck as possible. This will steady the brush and help control where the stain goes. Be careful not to get the stain anywhere but on the scratch. Blot any stray stain immediately with a rag. Let the stain dry.
7. Once the stain has dried, use a clean artist's brush to apply a coat of varnish or polyurethane. Be sure to choose a varnish or polyurethane that matches the finish already on your floor. Most finished floors are done in satin, but sometimes they can be glossier.
8. Once the first coat of varnish is dry, sand it very lightly with fine sandpaper. Wipe away any dust with a damp paper towel. Apply a second coat of varnish. Let dry.

Iron Out the Problem
Mend a Dent
Time: 20 to 45 minutes, depending on the floor and the depth of the dent

A friend once had a piano moved across her wood floor, and it left a long, deep dent behind it that made her feel as if her floor was ruined forever. Not true! Because wood is a naturally resilient product, dents can be fixed with a little patience, a hot iron, and some damp washcloths. She was playing a happy tune in no time.

What You Need
Two clean white terry washcloths
Steam iron
Paper towels

How to Get It Done
1. Dampen two white terry washcloths than have been washed in hot water. It's important to use extremely clean, freshly washed washcloths in this case because you want to make sure that any dyes or chemicals have been removed before using the towels on your floor.
2. Place the damp washcloths on the dent.
3. Set a steam iron to the cotton or hot setting. When the iron is hot, apply gentle pressure to the dent. Check it every 15 or 20 seconds to see how the dent is doing by lifting the washcloths. As one part of the dent is raised, move on to the next and so on. Dents in hardwood flooring will take longer to rise than those in soft wood flooring such as pine. But the damp washcloths and heat will eventually raise the dent, so be patient. Because the washcloths are thick and damp, the cotton setting will generally not burn them. However, if you do see the cloths darkening from the heat, switch to a new washcloth and keep working.
4. Once the dent has been removed, pat any damp part of the floor dry with a clean paper towel.

EXTRA! EXTRA!

When putting in a new floor, always have what contractors call "attic stock" on hand—an extra box of flooring to use for replacement and repair. Most contractors recommend buying 10 percent more than you need for any job.

Paint It!
Paint a Wood Floor
Time: Up to 3 days, depending on the number of rooms you are doing and variables in drying time

There are times when refinishing an old wooden floor is impossible or impractical. Maybe it's just too expensive, or the wood is so old that it just can't take another sanding. Or you might just love the look of painted wood floors. A friend painted the floors of her little weekend cottage recently for all three reasons: It would have cost too much to bring in a professional refinisher, the floorboards were very old and worn, and there was no guarantee that they would respond well to sanding, and she always wanted crisp, shiny white wooden floors. I was excited by her decision because I also knew it was a project she could do on her own. She was skeptical, but when I went through the process step-by-step, she realized it was doable and couldn't wait to get started.

My friend wanted super shiny floors, which meant she had to use high-gloss alkyd or oil-based enamel floor paint. However, if you want a softer look, you can use latex floor paint instead. A true gleam can only be achieved with oil paint, though. So check out samples at the home store before you buy.

What You Need
- Mop
- Sandpaper
- Wood putty
- Floor primer
- Paint tray
- Paint brushes
- Roller on extension rod
- Mask
- Rubber gloves
- Floor paint

How to Get It Done

1. Mop the floor clean.
2. Sand down any bumps or rough spots.
3. Fill any large knots, gouges, and gaps with wood putty. Sand the putty smooth when dry.
4. Cover the floor with a primer made specifically for floors and allow it to dry completely. Pour the primer into a paint tray. Begin by cutting in around the perimeter of the room with a paintbrush and then fill in the middle with a roller on an extension rod.
5. When the primer has dried, which could take up to 24 hours if you are using oil paint, paint the floor with your floor paint. Begin by cutting in around the perimeter of the room with a paintbrush and then fill in the middle with a roller.
6. Once the first coat of floor paint has dried completely (up to one day), check for any imperfections or obvious bumps or paint drops or blobs (it happens!). Sand them down with medium grit sandpaper and wipe away any dust with a very slightly damp cloth, then give the floor a second coat. If you are going over a very dark floor with a light paint, or a light floor with a dark paint, you may have to give the floor a third coat. If that's the case, wait for the second coat to dry completely, and paint with a third coat. It's best to wait 24 hours before moving furniture back in to make sure the floor is completely dry.

Note: Don't paint yourself into a corner! Move toward an exit!

SAFETY NOTES

If you use alkyd enamel paint, you must work in a well-ventilated room and wear a mask and rubber gloves.

**PEEL-AND-STICK
QUICK FIX**

The beauty of peel-and-stick tiles is that they are easy to put down and easy to place. If one of your peel-and-stick tiles gets damaged, simply soften the adhesive backing by running a hair dryer over the area until you can peel it up with a putty knife. Scrape the area down, making sure it is smooth and clean. Then simply peel the backing off your replacement tile and stick it down in place! Use a rolling pin to make sure full contact has been made and all of the air bubbles are rolled out.

The Great Pretenders: Vinyl and Laminates

I remember the vinyl floor in my childhood kitchen. It was easy to keep clean and practical, which was a good thing for my mom, considering that my sister, Caryn, and I were two very active and energetic girls. Vinyl, whether in sheets or tiles, can stand up to a busy family's comings and goings. It's quiet underfoot, water-resistant, inexpensive, and available in lots of colors and patterns. But it doesn't last as long as other flooring, and repairs on vinyl, while very doable, tend not to be as invisible as repairs on other floor material.

Peel-and-stick tile makes do-it-yourself projects possible. They offer a quick solution to recovering and refreshing the floor of a small bathroom, kitchen, or back entry, and the results buy you some time while you save for a sturdier flooring, such as stone or wood.

Vinyl can be printed with almost any pattern, emulating wood, stone, or brick. In the case of linoleum-like vinyl products, it can just be itself—a synthetic square in any range of colors and textures.

Laminates, on the other hand, take faux finishes one step further. Laminates have a dense fiberboard core with a paper pattern layer sealed under high-pressure both top and bottom with a plasticlike substance. That paper layer is usually a high-quality photograph of wood or stone. The best laminates can be very deceiving; they really can look like whatever they are pretending to be. Laminates are sold as planks and panels. Installation of laminates is different from other types of flooring material in that the planks are attached to each other and not to the floor itself. A vapor barrier, usually a sheet of plastic or foam, sits between the floor and the laminate planks, creating a "floating" system. Some laminate floating floors now come in a clicking system and don't require any glue. Instead of being glued together, the planks work on a tongue and groove system which fits together tightly and requires only minimal trimming with a utility knife to fit around corners and baseboards. That means you really can put a floating floor in yourself. Start small: Try a click-system laminate floor in a nursery-size bedroom or powder room.

Laminates have a lot going for them: They are virtually stainproof and fade-resistant, easy to clean, affordable, and comfortable to stand on for long periods. They can be susceptible to damage from excess moisture, so they are not the best bet in a child's bathroom. However, laminates, while pretty good at imitating wood or stone, will never have the natural beauty and character of the real thing.

A Square Deal
Replace a Vinyl Tile
Time: About 30 minutes

Replacing a damaged vinyl tile is even easier than patching a sheet vinyl floor.
Because the entire tile can be replaced, the "patch" will be invisible!

What You Need
Hair dryer

Putty knife

Vacuum

Vinyl adhesive

Notched trowel

Extra tile

Sponge

Rolling pin

How to Get It Done
1. Use a hair dryer to heat the damaged tile. This will soften the adhesive and make it easy for you to pry it up.
2. After prying off the tile, use a putty knife to scrape away any remaining adhesive. Use the hair dryer to soften any remaining adhesive. Vacuum the area to get every scrap up. You want the area to be as clean and smooth as possible.
3. Apply vinyl adhesive to the floor with a notched trowel.
4. Press the tile in place. Start at the center and work toward the edges to get out all the air bubbles.
5. Wipe any excess adhesive off the edges with a damp sponge.
6. Roll the patch with a rolling pin. Wipe the edges one more time to remove any excess adhesive.
7. Let the adhesive dry well before walking on the new tile.

Patch Things Up
Patch a Vinyl Floor
Time: About 40 minutes

I recently received a letter from a woman who said the vinyl floor in her kitchen tore after her husband dragged a sharp sheet of metal across it. She had been staring at the damage for more than a month. Clearly, no one was planning on repairing it, so she decided to give it a go herself and wrote to me for advice. This is the kind of letter I love because it gives me a chance to share exactly how to fix the tear *and* support her can-do attitude at the same time. Once the woman had gotten the rush that fixing her floor gave her, she was ready to conquer the world!

A successful patch in sheet vinyl can be made only if you have extra flooring on hand. Luckily, my pen pal had extra flooring in her basement. Most of the time, when you have sheet flooring installed, the installer will leave what's left behind. Don't throw it away. It's worth hanging onto in case you have to make a patch. The patch will not be invisible, but it's better than having a wounded floor.

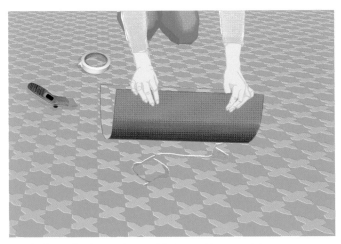

Step 2. Cover the damaged area with the patching material, matching the patterns.

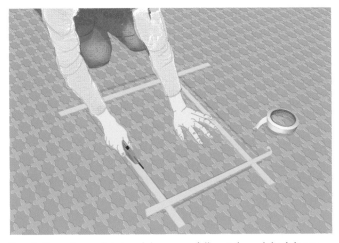

Step 4. Once the patch is taped down, carefully cut through both layers.

What You Need

Sharp straightedge utility knife
Extra piece of vinyl flooring
Masking or duct tape
Hair dryer
Putty knife
Vacuum
Vinyl adhesive
Notched trowel
Sponge
Rolling pin

How to Do It

1. Using a sharp straightedge utility knife, cut a piece of new vinyl flooring that is larger than the damaged area.
2. Cover the damaged area and line up the pattern of the patch with the pattern on the floor.
3. Tape the replacement piece over the damaged area with masking or duct tape to secure it in place.
4. Use the utility knife to cut through both layers of vinyl. Cut an area just larger than the damaged area so the hole and the patch will be exactly the same size.
5. Take the tape off and put the patch aside. Use a hair dryer to heat the damaged vinyl. This will soften the adhesive and make it easy for you to pry it up.
6. Use a putty knife to scrape away any remaining adhesive. Use the hair dryer to soften any remaining adhesive. Vacuum the area to get every scrap up. You want the area to be as clean and smooth as possible.
7. Apply vinyl adhesive to the floor with a notched trowel.
8. Press the patch in place. Start at the center and work toward the edges to get all the air bubbles out.
9. Wipe any excess adhesive off the edges with a damp sponge.
10. Roll over the patch with a rolling pin using your full body weight. Wipe the edges one more time to remove any excess adhesive.
11. Let the adhesive dry well before walking on the patch.

Step 6. Use a hair dryer to soften the adhesive.

Step 10. Roll over the area of the patch.

The Hard Stuff: Ceramic, Stone, and Porcelain

Stone and tile installation can seem pretty intimidating. It's true that creating a floor with heavy pieces of slate or marble might be best left to the pros, especially if you're just starting out on home improvement projects. But there are tiling projects that are within reach, such as replacing an old vinyl floor with tile. You'll get a professional, designer look with just a few basic skills!

For example, I recently added a bathroom to my home. While I certainly didn't do the complicated plumbing work myself, or the installation of the heavy shower basin, I did do several smaller jobs, including putting in the sink faucet (you'll read how in Chapter 6) and tiling the floor with a beautiful glass mosaic squares. The 1-inch squares come on 12- by 12-inch mesh sheets, which are easy to trim to size.

All floor-tiling projects should start with a clean slate. In my case, the bathroom floor was cement: There was no old flooring to remove, so I could get down to business pretty quickly. The toilet had yet to be installed, too. If you are replacing a

---

DEFINING MOMENT

CERAMIC TILE: For this type of tile, a mixture of clays are pressed into shape and fired at high temperatures. The bisque, or body, of ceramic tile may then be glazed or left unglazed.

GLAZED TILE: A glazed tile has a coating that is fired on after the tile has been fired once. It seals the tile (making it less prone to staining) and can give it a variety of finishes, from matte to high gloss.

GROUT: This thin mortar is used in masonry work to fill joints between bricks, blocks, and tiles.

PORCELAIN TILE: This is a type of tile made from a blend of fine-grain clays and other minerals to produce a very dense, hard product that is water and stain resistant. Porcelain tile will withstand years of heavy foot traffic both indoors and out and still look good.

THINSET MORTAR: This is the adhesive that you use to hold tiles in place. It's a mixture of cement and sand that is mixed with water.

UNGLAZED TILE: Unglazed tile has no surface coating. The color is the same on the face of the tile as it is on the back, resulting in very durable tiles that do not show the effects of heavy traffic. The most common unglazed tiles are red quarry tiles.

THE LOWDOWN ON THINSET

Thinset is the mortar adhesive that holds the tile in place. Manufacturers recommend different ways of mixing and using their products, so please follow directions provided by the maker for the specific brand you buy. Here are some general tips to keep your tiling on track.

- Use gray thinset if you plan to use gray or darker colored grout. Use white thinset if planning to use a light colored grout. Grout seals the seams and gives the floor a finished look. You can use thinset mortar as grout, or you can use a mortar product specifically designated as grout.
- Sanded thinset is a good choice for floors, especially those in wet areas like bathrooms and kitchens.
- Multipurpose and polymer-modified thinsets can be used for installing most ceramic tiles. Porcelain tiles benefit by being installed with latex-modified thinset.
- Mix only a small amount of thinset mortar at a time until you become used to its setting time, which will vary by region and climate.
- Allow at least 16 hours—ideally 24 hours—for the tile to set before walking on it.

floor in an existing bathroom, you must hire a plumber to remove the toilet first, then replace it when you are finished with the tiling job.

If you are replacing the vinyl in your bathroom, the old flooring has to come up. If you are removing sheet vinyl, use a sharp utility knife to cut around the perimeter of the room. Then cut the floor into four sections. Pry up a corner of each section and pull! You can do it. If it's stuck, use a hair dryer or heat gun to soften the adhesive backing. If you're removing vinyl tiles, pry them up with a putty knife and use the hair dryer to soften the glue. Scrape as much adhesive off the floor as you can, then vacuum.

A slam scraper or stand-up scraper, which is a wide blade attached to a long pole, gives you the leverage and sharpness you need to scrape up stubborn adhesive. You can rent one for less than $20 a day. Eventually, you'll have a vinyl-free floor. Ceramic or stone tile is thicker than vinyl so the saddles on the floor between rooms may have to be removed and replaced when you are finished the job.

Applying Style
Tile a Bathroom Floor with Mosaic Sheet Tiles
Time: 4 to 8 hours, plus drying time

Tiling is something that you may think is reserved for the pros. But if you read through these instructions carefully, gather all the materials together before you begin, and then go through this project step-by-step, *you can do it*. The secret is the mosaic sheets, which makes power cutting virtually unnecessary. If you are hesitant to try the project for the very first time on your very well-used bathroom floor, how about a less-conspicuous back entryway or mudroom floor? The process is exactly the same.

What You Need

Pry bar
Safety glasses
½-inch cement board (if the subfloor is wood)
1½-inch deck screws (if the subfloor is wood)
Utility knife
Thinset
Chisel
Tape measure
Pencil or chalk line

Floor tiles in sheets (be sure to buy 10 percent more than you need; your home store will help you calculate how much you need to buy)
Bucket for mixing thinset
Notched trowel
Plastic spacers
Large sponges
Tile grout
Grout float
Paper towels

How to Get It Done

1. If you are tiling an existing bathroom, you must remove the toilet first. You can hire a plumber to remove and replace it.

2. You may also have to remove baseboard molding from the room. Using a pry bar, gently pry off the pieces without breaking them so you can reinstall them when you're done. Remove all nails from the wood and use new nails when reinstalling.

3. Wear safety glasses at all times. Prepare the floor by cleaning it. If the subfloor is wood, apply ½-inch cement board, also known as backerboard, to the subfloor with 1½-inch deck screws every 8 inches. Deck screws are galvanized to protect from rust, so they are important to use in this job. To cut backerboard, score one side with a sharp utility knife and snap it. If you are applying the tile to a cement

floor, fill in any bellies, or indentations, in the cement with thinset. Chisel away any raised areas.

4. With a tape measure, find and mark the center of the room. Measure from the middle of the walls, front to back and side to side and mark each line with a pencil or chalk. When measuring, take cabinets and other permanently covered areas of the floor into consideration. The point at which the two lines meet in the center of the floor is your center mark.

5. Lay out the tiles in a dry run to see if you like the way they look and to see where you may need to cut the mesh backing. While it's impossible to determine what the final cuts will be, you can get a rough idea of where the tile sheets will need to be trimmed. Start at the center mark and work outward toward the walls.

6. Once you have found the arrangement you like, take up the tiles and prepare enough thinset in a bucket to cover about a quarter of the room. The thinset should be the consistency of peanut butter.

7. Trowel the thinset directly onto the floor with a notched trowel, pulling it toward you in an arc. Pulling the thinset toward you enables you to pick up any waste more easily and put it back into the bucket.

8. Carefully place the mosaic sheet on the thinset. Pressing too hard will squeeze the mortar out to the sides. Twist the tiles slightly into place. Set plastic spacers next to each tile to keep the tile rows evenly spaced. Place tiles on either side and then complete the next row until a quarter of the room is complete.

BARBARA'S BEST-KEPT SECRET

Preplanning the tile layout allows you to make sure that tile cuts are placed in the most inconspicuous edges of the room—behind the toilet or sink areas, for example.

Step 7. Trowel thinset directly on the floor.

Step 8. Place tile sheets directly on the thinset, but don't press down the tile too forcefully.

9. Wipe away any excess thinset with a barely damp sponge. Rinse the sponge.

10. Repeat steps 7 to 9 until the room is completely tiled. Using a clean sponge, wipe away as much excess thinset from the top of the tiles as you can.

11. Let the mortar set overnight.

12. Mix the grout to the consistency of cake mix. It should be looser than the thinset. Apply the grout with the grout float moving across the tile on the diagonal, pulling it toward you. Use light pressure to push the grout in between the tiles. Use the float to take away excess grout.

13. Wait about 20 minutes, before the grout is completely set, and wipe away as much excess grout as you can with a damp sponge. There should be as little grout on top of the tiles as possible. It is next to impossible to remove it once it dries.

14. Allow the grout to dry. The next day, polish off the grout "haze" from on top of the tiles with a paper towel.

Step 12. Apply the grout.

Tiling a floor is within your reach. And the beauty and value it adds
to your home makes learning tiling skills worth your while.

If It's Broken, Fix It
Replace a Broken Tile
Time: About 45 minutes

I have a girlfriend who loves to cook. When she gets going with pots and pans, *watch out*! She can really make a mess, but the end result is delicious. One evening she called me in tears. "Barbara, I have to replace my entire kitchen floor!" she cried. I gently asked her to slow down and tell me what had happened. In her haste, she had dropped a cast iron pot on her beautiful tile floor, and one of the tiles cracked. I'm not a gourmet like my friend, but I do love my kitchen, so I could definitely relate to my friend's distress: It's a drag when something you love gets damaged. But I reassured her that there is no reason to replace an entire tile floor if one or even four tiles have been cracked or broken. Removing a damaged tile and laying a new one is a straightforward do-it-yourself project, even for clumsy cooks!

What You Need

Hammer

Grout saw or a rotary tool with
  a cutting tip

Safety glasses

Hand towel

Work gloves

Wood or cold chisel

Vacuum

Matching replacement tile

Crayon (if you need to cut the
  replacement tile)

Manual tile cutter (if you need to cut
  the replacement tile)

Tile adhesive (for this job, you can
  use premixed adhesive, no need
  to mix thinset)

Putty knife

Notched trowel

Grout to match what's already
  on the floor

Grout float

Sponge

How to Get It Done

1. Isolate the damaged tile or tiles so that other tiles don't get damaged in the process. (It's likely that you'll have to break up the cracked or damaged tile with a hammer in order to get it out.) To protect the surrounding tiles from your hammer's shock waves, remove the grout that surrounds it with a grout saw. A grout saw is very inexpensive and easily found at any home improvement center or hardware store. Simply drag the saw blade through the grout. It will take

some time to cut all the way through (up to 20 minutes), but it's time well spent. You could also use a rotary tool with a cutting tip to take out the grout, but unless you already have one, a grout saw is cheaper and just as good. If you do use a rotary tool, use safety glasses.

2. Once you've removed all the grout around the damaged tile, lay a hand towel over the tile and hit it with a hammer until the tile is broken into 2-inch pieces. Put on your work gloves and remove the pieces. Discard them.

3. Use a wood or cold chisel to remove the adhesive from the floor. Take care not to gouge the floor or backerboard. Wear safety glasses to protect your eyes from any flying debris.

4. Vacuum up any small rubble. If the floor's not completely clean, the replacement tile won't adhere properly.

5. You should have one full box of extra tiles on hand (for just this sort of occasion) but if you don't, you can buy a new one. If you can't find an exact match, try to find one that closely resembles it. A slightly mismatched tile is better than a broken one.

6. If you are replacing a tile that has been cut to fit a space, measure it by taking the replacement tile and placing it on top of the area where the old tile was removed. Line up the edges by matching the tile pattern, if there is one, and use a crayon to mark the cut line. Use a manual tile cutter to make the cut along the line you made. It makes a series of cuts in the tile. You can then snap the tile (wear gloves and safety glasses) along the line.

7. In this situation, it's better to use premixed tile adhesive for the back of the new tile than trying to trowel adhesive onto the floor. Use a putty knife to "butter" the back of the tile with adhesive. Create even notches in the adhesive with the notched trowel.

8. Place the tile in the opening and tap it down gently with a hammer covered with the towel, or even better a rubber mallet. Be gentle; you don't want to break another tile! Make sure it is level with the other tiles.

9. Let it dry for 24 hours before applying grout.

10. Use a grout float to press the grout around the edges of the tile. Use a sponge to wipe the excess from the top of the tile. After about 30 minutes, wipe away any grout that has formed on the tile with a damp sponge. Wait another day before walking on it.

Carpet **tiles** are a great choice for do-it-yourself carpeting projects. You cannot install them over existing carpeting, but they can be easily placed over any other flat surface: a plywood subfloor, vinyl tile, wood, and even cement (making them a great way to transform a basement into liveable space). Several manufacturers offer carpet tiles in a range of colors and textures, so you are not limited as far as creating a look. Best of all, carpet tiles can be pulled up and taken with you to a new house or apartment. Most stick to the floor with little adhesive pads that allow the tiles to be moved around and rearranged. The biggest advantage carpet tiles offer is spot replacement. If a serious accident occurs (think sick puppy or spilled grape juice), you can simply pick up a tile and replace it with a new one.

Whatever kind of carpet you decide to buy, remember that regular maintenance will prolong its life and impart a good-as-new appearance. Follow the manufacturer's recommended cleaning methods. Vacuum regularly—at least twice a week—

DEFINING MOMENT

BERBER: Loop-pile carpet tufted with thick yarn, such as wool or olefin, berber is comfortable to walk on and creates a modern, informal look. Berber is now used loosely to describe many level or multilevel loop carpeting.

BINDING: This is a band of fabric sewn over a carpet edge to protect, strengthen, or decorate it.

BROADLOOM: This is carpet produced in widths wider than 6 feet. Standard broadloom is usually 12 feet wide.

DENSITY: The density is the amount of pile yarn in the carpet and the closeness of the tufts. In general, the denser the pile, the better the performance.

HAND: This term is used to describe how carpeting feels when you run your hand over it: smooth, textured, velvety, and so on.

PILE: This is the surface of carpet, also called the face or nap.

PLUSH: A smooth-textured carpet in which individual tufts are only minimally visible and the overall visual effect is that of a single level of yarn ends is sometimes called "velvet-plush."

PLY: Here single carpet yarn ends have been ply-twisted together to form a plied yarn, e.g. two-ply or three-ply.

SAXONY: In this cut-pile carpet texture with twisted yarns in a relatively dense, erect configuration, the effect is well-defined tuft tips.

SISAL: Originally made of vegetable fibers, carpet has recently attained the look of natural sisal with softer synthetic alternatives. Wool and synthetic alternatives are almost worry-free and offer a variety of interesting textures, patterns, and prints.

TILES: A relatively new product, carpet tiles usually come with the carpet pad attached and ready to install. Carpet tiles are made in a variety of patterns and textures, including shag and Berber styles.

TUFTED: Most broadloom carpeting is tufted. Continuous strands of yarn are stitched into a primary backing. A latex coating locks the loops in place. Then a secondary backing is applied for strength and durability.

to remove loose soil and dust. Vacuuming will never hurt your carpet if done properly because it ensures dirt doesn't get embedded in the carpet and ruin the fibers. Have a professional deep-clean your rug once a year.

Out, Damned Spot!

Most carpet available today is stain-resistant (but not stainproof), which means that many (but not all) spills can be removed . . . if you act fast. The longer you wait to take care of an accident, the greater the chance that it will become a permanent part of your carpet. Check with the carpet manufacturer for their specific recommendations. Here are some easy, old-fashioned ways I use to deal with common stains using ingredients you probably already have on hand. I'm not sure who came up with these ideas, but I remember my mom using these techniques to deal with carpet mishaps. Remember to always pretest any solvent in an inconspicuous area before you use it on the actual stain.

INK

Solvent: rubbing alcohol Apply rubbing alcohol to a clean white cloth, white paper towel, or cotton ball. If the spot extends deep into the pile, use a blotting motion until the spot is removed or no color is transferred to the cloth. Do not allow the alcohol to penetrate into the backing because this will destroy the latex bond. If the spot is on the surface only, rub in one direction at a time. Never use a circular motion to remove a spot because this may destroy the texture. Stop if the spot is removed. If not, go to the next step.

Apply a small quantity of detergent solution to the spot. To make the detergent solution, mix ¼ teaspoon of a hand dishwashing detergent that does *not* contain lanolin or bleach with 1 quart of water. Use a blotting motion to work the detergent into the affected area. If the spot is being removed, continue applying detergent and blotting with a white paper towel until the spot is removed.

Rinse with tap water using a spray bottle, and blot to remove excess moisture.

Spray lightly with water, do not blot this time; apply a pad of paper towels and allow the area to dry.

If there is still some stain on the carpet, moisten the tufts in the stained area with 3 percent hydrogen peroxide. Let it stand for an hour. Blot and repeat until the carpet is stain free. Light will cause peroxide to change back to water so no rinsing is necessary.

CARING FOR YOUR VACUUM

With these simple steps in mind, your vacuum should serve you well for many years.

- Follow the vacuum cleaner manufacturer's instructions.
- Change the vacuum bag when it becomes more than half full. As the bag becomes full, efficiency is reduced.
- Keep the vacuum brushes and hoses clean and free of debris.
- Inspect belts to make certain they are working properly
- Always keep a spare belt for replacement.

RED WINE

Solvent: equal parts dishwashing liquid and hydrogen peroxide Spray or dab the mixture on the stain. Blot with a paper towel. Because peroxide is a bleaching agent, the remedy could potentially bleach some colored rugs. Always test a small inconspicuous patch before using it on the stained area.

WAX

Solvent: denatured alcohol First, scrape away as much wax as you can. Then place a sheet of butcher paper, glossy side up, or a portion of a brown paper bag on top of the wax. Press the tip of a warm iron gently over the affected area until the wax melts and attaches to the paper. Lift the paper from the carpet. Dab a small amount of denatured alcohol onto the stain if any candle dye is left on the carpet. Rinse with water.

Fire the Damage
Fix a Burn
Time: About 45 minutes, not including tape setting time

If the burn is small and on the very top or surface of the carpet, you can improve the situation by carefully clipping off blackened ends of tufts with small, sharp scissors. Trim the surrounding tufts to minimize indentation.

If the burn is more severe and has penetrated the carpet, you will have to remove and patch the section with a spare piece of carpeting. You can remove a piece from a closet or other inconspicuous place or use extra you may have saved. The technique can also be used for stubborn stains that resist removal.

What You Need
Spare carpeting
Sharp utility knife
Tape measure
Work gloves
Vacuum
Double-sided carpet tape
Books

How to Get It Done
1. Use a tape measure to measure about 1 inch all around the burn and use that as a measure to cut a patch. Using a sharp utility knife, cut a patch of spare carpeting into a square or rectangle, depending on the size of the burn.
2. Put on work gloves, and cut a piece of the burned area the same size as the patch with the utility knife. Remove the carpet using the patch as a guide.
3. Vacuum the area.
4. Cover the hole with double-sided carpet tape. Press the patch into place and weight it overnight with a pile of books.
5. Vacuum it again to blend the seams.

Your floors are fixed, and you did it yourself. Let's roll out the welcome mat and see just how much you can do to repair, enhance, and improve your windows and doors. Quite a bit, actually!

Chapter 4
Windows (and Doors) of Opportunity

Natural light and fresh air are *so* important to me. I love to feel and see the sun streaming in through my bedroom windows in the morning. My son, Zachary, and I often watch how the sky changes as the sun sets, and these are moments I treasure. Cool breezes on a summer evening brings out my romantic side, and listening to rain drops as they hit my windowpanes is both calming and meditative. These are just a few reasons why windows and doors are so important to me.

Windows and doors are also integral parts of a home's structure. They play an important role in controlling light, ventilation, and temperature. Windows and doors can also be architecturally beautiful as well as functional. If you're upgrading windows, choose a style that matches your needs both practically and stylistically. For example, casement windows scream modern, while double-hung windows with 12 panes over 12 panes say traditional. The wrong windows can make a house look awkward or off balance, but properly chosen windows beautifully placed can make even the simplest ranch or cape "best of class." Windows should be placed to create balance and harmony on the exterior of a house, as well as to take advantage of the best views and light inside the home.

Exterior doors should be sturdy and well made, with good quality, attractive locks strong enough to keep intruders out, while offering style and substance inside. Exterior doors can be solid or windowed, simply chic or lavishly ornate. Either way, they should fit in with the style of your home and welcome guests.

Like doors to the outside, interior doors should be strong, close properly, and blend well with the style and décor in your home. If you don't love the doors inside your house, you can change them without replacing them. The simplest hollow core, solid core, or luaun veneer doors can be transformed with paint, by adding molding and decorative trim, or by changing knobs and other hardware.

Maintenance is essential when it comes to doors and windows. Sticky windows and wobbly doorknobs are annoying to deal with and potentially dangerous. Simple repairs and upgrades can make a big difference in your home and in your ability to tackle other, more challenging projects.

Choosing and caring for doors and windows is an open-and-shut case, so let's get started.

SAFETY NOTES

Remember to always follow manufacturer's instructions when using any product or tool, even if you've used it in the past. Manufacturers take a lot of time to write user-friendly instructions, and they know better than anyone about how to use their particular material or tool. Also remember when embarking on any window or door project to work in any area that has been cleared of debris or any breakable or movable objects. When you are working with saws or other power tools, wear safety glasses and gloves. Follow product instructions. When working with paints or solvents of any kind, make sure the room is well ventilated. Wear a mask and safety glasses for protection against fumes and dust. Please dispose of solvents in a way that complies with local environmental rules.

DEFINING MOMENT

ALUMINUM: Aluminum windows are more durable than unclad wood. They're also light and easy to handle. They are insulated with a thermal break of extruded vinyl and sometimes foam, which reduces heat loss and condensation. Aluminum windows get a top finish that protects from corrosion but will deteriorate in salty air, making them a less desirable choice for seaside homes.

CLAD WOOD: Many wood windows are covered with durable aluminum or vinyl. This cladding is available in several colors and helps to keep windows virtually maintenance-free for years. Neither coating requires painting, and aluminum and vinyl coating will not rust or rot.

UNCLAD WOOD: Wood windows are beautiful, easily painted, and affordable. Wood doesn't conduct cold or allow for condensation, but it can shrink and swell so wood windows will warp and rot over time unless they're protected. Wood windows typically come unfinished so if you want to paint, purchase them with preprimed frames. Some manufacturers offer prepainted windows in standard colors such as white, green, and black. If you choose to stain windows, a weather- and water-resistant topcoat is necessary. Exterior grade polyurethane will do the trick.

VINYL: Vinyl windows are made from rigid, impact-resistant polyvinyl chloride (PVC), with hollow spaces inside to make them resistant to heat loss and condensation. Inexpensive vinyl windows can warp or bend when exposed to extremes of heat and cold (those in the Northeast take heed), making them hard to operate. They can also leak air. Vinyl windows can't be painted, and darker colors may fade over time.

First Glass
Replace a Broken Windowpane
Time: About 1 hour

When one of Zachary's friends hit a baseball through one of my windows, I had to replace it. I think Zach was more upset than I was!

What You Need

Work gloves

Safety glasses

Chisel

Heat gun or hair dryer

Hammer

Flat head screwdriver

Tape measure

New glass

Glazing points

Glazing putty

Putty or glazing knife

Paint

How to Get It Done

1. Be sure to wear gloves and safety glasses. Remove the old glass carefully. With a chisel, chip out the old glazing, which is the putty around the window that helps hold it in place, and glazing points, little metal triangles that also hold the window in place, until you can remove the glass. Softening the glazing with a heat gun or hair dryer may make it easier to remove. If the window is broken or the glass is missing entirely, remove all glazing from the frame. On some old windows you may need to remove the wood glazing stop. Carefully pry one side up at a time using a hammer and flat head screwdriver. If the frame breaks, replace it with a new one or use glazing putty when replacing the glass.

2. Using a tape measure, measure the opening in the frame and subtract ⅛ to 3/16 of an inch from the vertical and horizontal measurements. You don't want to have to jam the glass tightly into the opening. Your hardware store or home improvement center can cut new glass to your specifications.

3. Set the new piece of glass into the frame. Do not press too hard against the glass or you may break it. Use at least two glazing points on each side (more if the opening is larger than 12 by 12 inches). Work the glazing putty around the glass and the frame using a putty or glazing knife. Do not open the window until the glaze hardens (at least 24 hours).

4. Paint the glazing following the manufacturer's directions.

Storm of the Century
Install Storm Windows
Time: About 1 hour per window

Insulating windows in the cold weather months is the best way to keep warm and lower your heating bills. That's an unbeatable combination especially because fuel prices are apt to fluctuate upward rather than downward. So when October rolls around, I start installing storm windows in my house. It's still warm enough to work outside comfortably, and by the time I'm done, I know I'm all set for winter months to come.

Storm windows are available in double- or triple-track systems. These systems, often called "combination" windows, are sliding units that attach to the outside of your existing windows. Double-track windows have an inside track for the lower glass, which allows it to slide up or down. The upper glass and the screen share the outside track. Triple-track windows have three channels, which allow both upper and lower glass as well as screens to slide up and down. The middle channel holds the screen panel; the two outer channels hold the glass panels. The panels are accessed from the inside of the main window.

You can also create makeshift "storm windows" using heat-shrink plastic film that can insulate from inside or outside your house. Most home centers sell plastic film that stops drafts effectively by using heat to shrink the film, making a tight, wrinkle-free, and nearly invisible seal.

Depending on what method you choose, follow these simple guidelines for draft-free winter windows.

What You Need

Storm windows in the appropriate size to fit your windows or a heat-shrink plastic film kit for indoors or outdoors
6-in-1 interchangeable screwdriver
Screws
Caulk

4-in-1 level
Double-sided tape
10- or 25-foot tape measure
Scissors
Hair dryer

How to Get It Done

DOUBLE- OR TRIPLE-TRACK

1. Attach the storm window units to the side of the house using screws through the predrilled screw holes in the flanges.
2. Caulk between the mounting flanges and the window to which they are attached. Don't caulk the small holes at the bottom of the unit. These holes are designed to allow condensation to escape.
3. Be sure the units are level and that the frames are not distorted by overtightening the screws through the flanges. If the frames are distorted, you will not be able to move the sashes up and down easily.

INSIDE-MOUNTED MAKESHIFT STORM WINDOWS

1. Be sure to read the manufacturer's directions before applying the plastic film you've selected.
2. Clean your window trim.
3. Apply double-sided tape around the inside of the window.
4. Measure with a tape measure and cut the film approximately 2 inches larger than the window.
5. Remove the protective paper from the double-sided tape and attach the tape to the film. Begin at the top of the window and move clockwise, pressing the film against the tape.
6. Use a hair dryer, as directed by the manufacturer, to shrink the film.

OUTSIDE-MOUNTED MAKESHIFT STORM WINDOWS

1. These plastic film kits for outside use may attach with tacking strips or may have plastic moldings that can be permanently attached and allow you to remove or replace the film as necessary. Follow the manufacturer's directions for installation.
2. Clean the window trim for best adhesion.
3. Cut the molding strips and use 45-degree miters at the corners of the windows.
4. Attach the molding to the windows with double-sided tape and use the tape to temporarily hold the plastic to the molding.
5. Snap the moldings into place over the plastic. Starting at the top, move clockwise around the window, holding the plastic film tight to prevent wrinkling.

BARBARA'S BEST-KEPT SECRET

You can leave external film or combination storm windows in place during the summer to decrease air-conditioning costs, or you can remove and store them until the next winter.

If your windows are narrow, you can give the illusion of a wider expanse by placing the drapery brackets 3 to 6 inches away from the edge of the window. The curtains will look as if they are covering additional windows, and the extra fabric gives the room a luxurious, dramatic feel.

OPPOSITE: Measuring windows is a breeze, especially if you have an ace assistant!

Full Window Fashion

Window treatments such as drapes, curtains, sheers, and swags can make a dramatic difference in the way your rooms look with very little effort on your part. Tired of looking at the brick wall facing your kitchen window, or worse, your neighbor's trash collection? Simple café curtains made from vintage or new tea towels clipped to tension rods take just minutes to make and instantly hide unpleasant or uninspiring views.

Hanging drapery rods takes a bit more planning, but still, in less than 45 minutes, you'll be on your way to transforming a blah family room into a dramatic backdrop for your favorite soirées. And drapes don't have to be expensive. Let your imagination run wild: Inexpensive Indian bedspreads, sari fabric, vintage yardage, and even sheets can be repurposed into drapes and curtains. Ready-made curtains can be altered for a custom look. I did that, and it not only resulted in unique, one-of-a-kind floor length curtains, but it also made my ceiling and windows look higher in the process.

First, I found some sheer drapes in a natural color that fit the wall of large windows and glass sliding doors leading out to my backyard. I installed the curtain rod a couple of inches above the window and door frames. Then I hung the drapes, and . . . they looked okay. I lived with the drapes while I thought about the problem. (I find it's a good idea to step back and think about something before I rush to change it.) I wanted to give myself some time to solve this problem *once* instead of having to redo it several times. Then it hit me: If I moved the rod much closer to the ceiling, the ceiling and windows would appear taller and more elegant. Of course, that would mean I would either have to buy new drapes (the ones I just bought didn't meet the floor when hung from the top of the wall) or I would have to figure out a way to alter them so they were longer.

The solution: a wide, luxurious hem in a coordinating fabric attached to the bottom of the existing drape. All I needed was a few yards of scrumptious silk.

After moving the drapery rod closer to the ceiling (it's easy—I'll show you how in "Move a Curtain Rod to Make Windows Appear Larger" on page 112), I measured the distance between the top of the hem on the drape (which would be cut off in my case because the sewing line would show if I tried taking out the hem) and the floor. It was about 20 inches. The fabric was simply sewn along the bottom of the drapes. It was just a simple modification, but what an enormous difference it made in the room.

Door Prize

Doors are pretty simple—usually a rectangular panel of some kind of material (wood, fiberglass) that helps us access buildings and rooms and close off closets or other storage areas. I think doors are a neglected part of a room—people seem to forget that their surface offers opportunity for paint and other embellishments. Changing your door's color, finish, and general appearance can bring a room's décor together. Changing the door itself can represent a major upgrade to your home. For example, replacing inexpensive hollow-core doors with wood raised-panel doors can make a huge difference in the appearance, desirability, and value of your home. Even switching conventional brass-finish door knobs with stylish nickel-plated versions can transform your door's personality! So don't forget about your doors when embarking on a renovation or decorating project.

Exterior Doors

The front door is one of the first things people see when they come to your home. It makes a statement and sets the tone for the rest of the house. Your door should say, "Come on in!" rather than "Keep out!" To convey a sense of friendly warmth, a front door should be freshly painted or stained. Door handles and hardware should be polished, not tarnished. House numbers should be clearly visible from the street. Accessories such as the mailbox and doorbell should coordinate with door hardware and must be in good working order. Ample lighting is a must: One overhead light or sconces flanking the door are true beacons for homecomings.

Trash containers, bicycles, toys, and other stray stuff can be relegated to the garage or backyard. Make your front door even more welcoming with inexpensive accessories that say "Hello" in the most charming way. Wind chimes, flowers in containers or window boxes (in winter months, a small evergreen in a large pot adds life), and a place to sit such as a wicker chair, wooden bench, or rocker bring curb appeal right to your doorstep.

A brand new front door can also make the façade of your house look brand new. If your replacement is wood, ask for core-block construction. Core-block doors are made from layers of laminated wood blocks, which are then covered with veneer. The direction of the wood grain on the blocks alternates, so core-block doors are

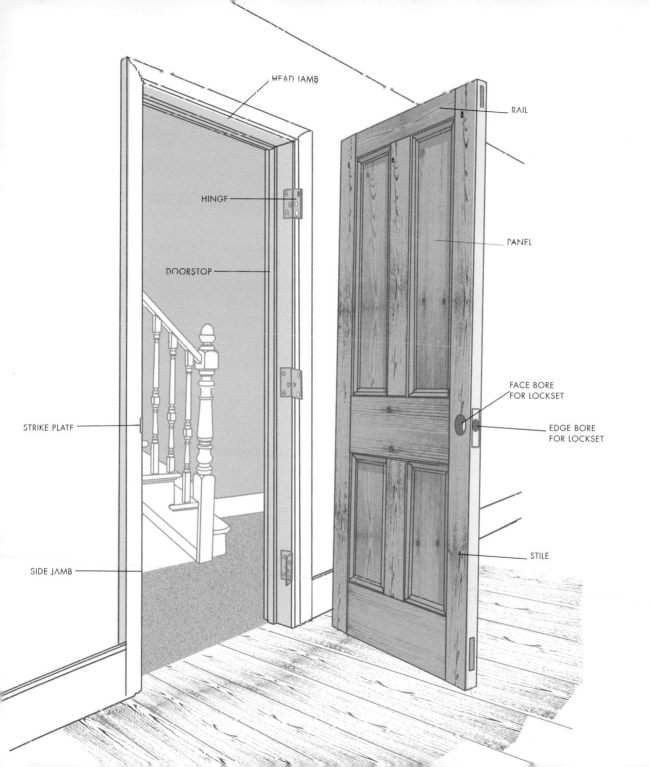

HEAD JAMB

RAIL

HINGE

PANEL

DOORSTOP

FACE BORE
FOR LOCKSET

EDGE BORE
FOR LOCKSET

STRIKE PLATE

STILE

SIDE JAMB

115

less likely to warp than solid-core doors. Alternatively, exterior wooden doors can be made of solid wood using frame and panel construction to counteract the effects of climatic or seasonal changes.

Wood doors can be painted or stained. If painting, consider using high-gloss alkyd paint for an elegant but easy-to-clean finish.

Steel doors have energy-efficient foam-core insulation and are fully weather stripped by the manufacturer. They resist shrinking, swelling, and warping. Their tough steel construction withstands extreme weather with little maintenance. Steel doors come preprimed and ready to paint any color you like. Many steel doors come primed with a rust-resistant finish. "Raw" steel doors need to be primed first with a rust-resistant primer and then painted.

Fiberglass doors offer the same energy-saving and easy installation qualities as steel doors. Fiberglass doors sometimes have a molded wood grain texture so they give the appearance of a real wood door when painted or stained. Yes, you can stain a fiberglass door! Fiberglass is also highly weather-, scratch-, and dent-resistant. This makes a fiberglass door a great choice for busy family homes in extreme climates. One caveat: Fiberglass doors (and windows) are expensive.

Interior Doors—The Inside Story

Interior doors give us privacy and, with the help of walls, define spaces in a home. We don't think a lot about our inside doors unless they're stuck or squeaking. But doors can add to the decorative statement your house makes. And while replacing interior doors is a job for serious do-it-yourselfers, you can do a lot to enhance the doors you already have (and keep them from sticking while you're at it).

Many of my friends, especially those who live in city apartments, have plain wood veneer or luaun doors. They have a tendency to look cookie-cutter drab in as-is brown. A lick of semigloss paint brightens them up in no time. Picture frame molding, miter-cut to form corners, and applied to the door in one, two, or three rectangles with glue and tack nails, can be painted to resemble traditional raised panel doors. These panels can be lined with a bit of padding and fabric to add richness and texture to a door. In fact, the insets of genuine panels doors can also be enhanced with fabric, leather, grass cloth, or other materials. Decorative panels attached or set into a plain-Jane door add a hand-crafted look.

I found some beautiful carved wood panels at a national import store. They were *very* inexpensive but I knew they would be elevated to artisan status when set into my plain, flat closet doors. It's an easy woodworking project that results in a very expensive designer look. I bought four panels for each of the four doors of my closet. You can try the same technique with your closet doors, as long as they have a solid core or solid wood framing (such as louvered closet doors—the center slats can be easily cut out). If you're stuck with hollow core doors, consider placing light-weight decorative panels or wood trim to the front using wood glue, finish nails, or small L-brackets. Attach with wood screws and a screwdriver.

DEFINING MOMENT

HOLLOW-CORE DOORS: Hollow-core doors are made from two thin veneer plywood or hardboard faces. Interior cardboard supports help keep the door rigid. Hollow-core doors are light-weight and inexpensive, provide a smooth surface for paint or stain, and are easily installed or replaced. The cons? They're easy to damage and are ineffective as sound barriers.

MDF DOORS: Solid medium-density fiberboard (MDF) is an engineered wood product that is produced in sheets and then milled like hardwood. It is extremely dense and heavy with a flat, smooth surface that takes paint beautifully. It's highly sound-resistant, sturdy, and very affordable.

SOLID-CORE DOORS: Solid-core doors are made from high-density fiberboard or hardboard. A top-quality solid-core door will also have hardwood support where screw holes are located for good adhesion without stripping. These doors, like solid wood doors, come in raised panel and flat-panel styles. They can be stained or painted.

SOLID WOOD DOORS: High-quality wood doors can be very expensive. Not only is solid hardwood expensive, but wood doors also take time to manu-facture because they must be kiln- and air-dried to prevent warping or cracking. Joints must be carefully manu-factured to withstand stress. However, you can find old wood doors at antique stores and salvage yards. Old doors are often well made, but because door sizes were not standardized until the middle of the 20th century and some-times not even then, vintage wood doors will most likely have to be modi-fied and retrofitted by a carpenter in order to fit for your openings. However,

this could still be less expensive than buying brand new wood doors.

INSWING (I/S): A door that opens in.

OUTSWING (O/S): A door that opens out.

LEFT HAND: When you look at the door from the outside, I/S door hinges are on the left, and O/S door hinges are on the right.

RIGHT HAND: When you look at the door from the outside, I/S door hinges are on the right, and O/S door hinges are on the left.

LITE: This is a pane of glass in a door.

DIVIDED LITE: These panes of glass are or appear to be divided.

GRILLE: This is a plastic, wooden, or metal grid that is applied on top of solid glass to give a door (or window) the appearance of divided lites.

Door Redo
Transform Interior Solid-Core Doors with Decorative Panels
Time: 1 day, including painting and drying time

It's really very easy to jazz up a dull interior solid-core door. Here's how.

What You Need

2 sawhorses

2 2×4s at least 1 foot longer than the door

Solid-core door

Screwdriver or power drill with screwdriver bits

Decorative panels with at least a ½-inch frame for setting into door

Pencil

Reciprocating jigsaw

Power drill

½-inch, L-shaped picture frame molding to fit around the outside of the panel

16 small rectangular metal braces

32 1-inch screws

Primer

Paint

Paintbrushes

How to Get It Done

1. Set up the sawhorses and lay the two 2×4s across them to hold the door as you work.
2. Remove the door by unscrewing the hinges. Save all the hinge hardware so you can reinstall the door when the panels are in place.
3. Decide on the placement of your panel: I wanted mine centered. You can also place the panel slightly higher, leaving a wider area at the bottom of the door. It's completely up to you.
4. Lay the door and the panel flat on the floor and trace around the panel with a pencil.
5. Lay the door across the 2×4s on the two sawhorses. Make sure the 2×4s support the door on either side.

I stapled fabric on the back of the open panels to add color and texture—and to hide my clothes from view.

Opposite: Measure twice and cut once!

My finished closet doors are one of a kind, and I "made" them myself!

6. Cut out the marked area of the door with a reciprocating jigsaw. Start the cut by drilling a small hole on the inside corner of the traced area and cutting down one long side of the marked area. It is essential that you allow for ⅛ inch top to bottom and left to right (¹⁄₁₆ inch on each side). A simple way to do this is to "take the line" when cutting, which means cut through the trace line you made.

7. Don't let the center fall out because it might tear the veneer off the door. As soon as you are finished cutting the long side of the panel, slide the door over so the 2×4 is supporting the cut side. Then cut the other long side. When that cut is finished, slide the other 2×4 underneath. Proceed with the top and bottom cuts.

8. Remove the panel you have cut. Now you have a door with a big rectangular hole in the middle!

9. Fit the decorative panel into the opening. It should be slightly smaller than the opening.

10. Create a ledge for the decorative panel to sit on by attaching the picture frame molding to the back of the door by screwing in four metal braces. One should be placed in every corner, and another one should be placed in the middle of each side.

11. Now it is time to paint the door, brackets, and molding. It will be difficult to paint them once the decorative panel is installed, unless you are painting that as well. In that case, you can prime and paint everything at the end. I didn't want to paint my panels, however.

12. Allow the primer and paint to dry completely (about 3 hours).

13. Now you can install the panel. Drop the panel into the opening you made. It should fit snuggly on the ledge you created with the molding.

14. Attach the panel with the four remaining metal braces, with one in the middle of each side. Attach them on the same side as the other braces you installed earlier. Touch up the braces with a bit of paint.

15. Reinstall the door.

That's the Rub
Fix a Door That's Rubbing
Time: About 20 minutes

A rubbing door does *not* have to be an annoying fact of life. This quick fix will get rid of rubs forever.

What You Need

Screwdriver

Toothpick

Hammer

Finish nail

Nail set (if you need to touch up the door frame)

Wood putty (if you need to touch up the door frame)

Paint (if you need to touch up the door frame)

How to Get It Done

1. Check and tighten all hinge screws to determine where the door is rubbing (top, middle, or bottom). If it is rubbing on top, loosen the top hinge screws about halfway (do not remove). If it is rubbing on the bottom, do this to the bottom hinge. Take a toothpick and slide it behind the hinge on the side toward the center of the doorjamb and tighten the screws.

2. If the door is still rubbing, locate the area of damaged paint on the doorjamb. Take your hammer and finish nail and nail into the wood between the doorstop and jamb edge until the nail is set.

3. If you are planning on retouching the doorjamb after you have adjusted the door, make sure to use a nail set to sink the nail below the surface of the wood. Fill in the shallow hole with wood putty for a completely smooth surface for your paint touch-up.

Door Magic
Open a Locked Door without a Key
Time: 1 minute

Once not too long ago, a friend of Zach's locked himself in our bathroom. He panicked, but I didn't. I had him out in a minute, without damaging my door. I wiped away his tears and gave him some milk and cookies, and all was right with the world.

What You Need
Paper clip or bobby pin
Allen wrench or hex key

How to Get It Done
If the doorknob has a small hole in the center of the handle, simply insert a long, skinny object such as a paper clip that's been straightened out and push hard. When the object hits the inside, continue to push while turning the handle until the door opens. Be sure to unlock the door once you have it open. You can also use a thin Allen wrench or hex key for this.

Safe House
Install a Surface-Mounted Lock
Time: About 30 minutes

A surface-mounted lock, which can be purchased at your local home improvement center or hardware store, is a simple way to make your home even safer by providing an extra layer of protection against intruders.

What You Need
Surface-mounted lock
Pencil
Utility knife
Power drill with screwdriver bits

How to Get It Done
1. Position the lock on the door at the height you want. A good place to put a surface-mounted lock is a few inches above the existing doorknob. Mark the holes on the lock with a pencil. Place the part that receives the chain or bolt on the door frame trim and lightly trace the outer edges of it in pencil. Use your utility knife to cut away the door trim until you reach the doorjamb. Replace the receiving piece and mark the screw hole with a pencil.
2. Use your drill and a bit that is slightly smaller than the mounting screw. Drill shallow holes at all the pencil marks. These are your pilot holes for the screws. Align the lock with the pilot holes and use your screwdriver to place and tighten all the screws (never overtighten or you will run the risk of stripping the screws).

Knob Appeal
Replace a Locking Doorknob
Time: About 30 minutes

If you've moved into a new home, you probably will want to change the locks. Or if your front or back doorknobs have become uncooperative, you may want to install new ones. Either way, the result will be a more secure, better functioning, and more attractive door.

Doorknobs are dual-function jewelry for your door: They provide visual interest and beauty while helping to keep you secure, so when choosing a new doorknob set, select the best and sturdiest you can afford. They come in a wide range of metals and finishes, from brass to brushed nickel. The knobs themselves come in lots of shapes and sizes, including traditional round, oval, and octagon, and some have lever handles. If you pick something you really love, you'll be even more motivated to install it right away.

Because different doorknobs function in different ways, be sure to choose a knob that works the way you want it to. Choose the kind of knob that suits the needs of your family. For example, lever handles are easy for older people and children to grab. Round and oval knobs may be more difficult for little hands to use. Most sets will come with mechanical drawings and clear instructions, but here's what you can expect.

What You Need
Screwdriver
Doorknob and lock set
Matching strike plate (if the set doesn't come with one)

How to Get It Done
1. Detach the knob trim (the ring of metal between both doorknobs and the door) by removing the two screws that hold it on. Sometimes the knob trim has to be gently pried off with a flat head screwdriver rather than unscrewed.
2. Remove two more screws under the trim. These long screws attach the doorknobs on either side of the door.
3. Pull the doorknobs apart and remove them from the door.

4. Remove the two screws that hold the bolt (the locking mechanism), which remains attached to the door, and extract the bolt.

5. Now is the time to make sure the metal strike plate attached to the frame around the door (this is the metal piece that catches the bolt) matches the new knobs. If the strike plate is in good condition and matches the finish of your new doorknob, make sure the screws are holding it securely in place. If it doesn't match (it's brass tone and your new knob set is silver), unscrew it and replace it with a matching plate. Your kit may not have this piece; if it doesn't, you can pick up one at the hardware store.

6. Insert the new bolt into the door and screw it into place. The slanted side should face the direction that the door closes.

7. Place the new knob trim piece between one new doorknob and the door, and insert the doorknob.

8. Insert the other knob and trim piece on the other side of the door. Make sure the two are aligned so that the long screws hold them together.

9. Tighten the screws gradually, alternating sides so that each comes together uniformly.

The process for changing an interior locking door is the same for an exterior doorknob that locks with a key.

Slide into Style
Install Sliding Closet Doors
Time: About 40 minutes

New closet doors are a quick and easy way to give a tired room a fresh new look. If you're dealing with a very wide doorway, look for sliding doors that have their wheels on the track that is attached to the floor and use the upper track as a guide only. Otherwise, simply measure your old doors and take the measurements with you to a lumberyard or home improvement center. Consider the room in which you will be using the doors and select a style that suits your décor. Decide whether you want finished or unfinished doors and if you choose unfinished, apply paint or stain before hanging the doors.

Many sliding closet doors can be removed by pulling them up, out, and off the upper track.

What You Need

Safety glasses

Power drill with screwdriver bits, or screwdriver

Sliding closet doors with track hardware

10- or 25-foot tape measure

Hacksaw (if needed to size the new track)

Hammer

Nail

How to Get It Done

1. Lift the old doors up and out of the track. Most ride in the overhead track, some have a small lever that you hold down to release them from the track, while others have cutouts along the track where the rollers can be lifted free. Put on your safety glasses because you will be looking up while working on the hardware that is above your head. Use your power drill or screwdriver to remove the screws holding the overhead track in place. You will not need to save any of the old hardware. Remove the bottom brackets.

2. Measure the new track hardware against the old for length. Use your hacksaw to size the new track, if necessary. Install the upper track. If you are using the old screw holes for the new track, go ahead and install the screws. (It's helpful to have a friend hold it in position while you do this.) If the new track has a different placement, use your drill, or a hammer and nail, to position pilot holes to guide the new screws in. Be sure the screws are well seated, so the heads don't interfere with the movement of the door, but don't overtighten them because this can warp the track.

3. Place the bottom track on the floor and hang first the back, then the front sliding door. Let the doors hang to find the center for the bottom track, then remove the doors. Mark the position of the lower track on the doorjamb, then mark each screw hole along the floor. Attach the lower track, and then rehang the doors—again starting with the back door. Attach the doors to the lower track and slide them gently back and forth. Enjoy the silent glide of your new closet doors.

Now that your doors and windows look beautiful and are operating smoothly (and you did it yourself!), let's tackle lights and lighting. After all, you can't enjoy the work you've done so far if you can't see it clearly!

properly. Electrifying pretty Chinese hanging lamps and suspending them from the ceiling turns a ho-hum living room into a romantic refuge. Lighting projects like these are easy. I've done many myself, so I know you can do them, too.

The principles of lighting make a lot of sense and are not as hard to learn as you may think. And once you understand the basics, you can begin to experiment! Move lamps around, add candles, lower the wattage of bulbs, and use bulbs with different tints (light pink, flat white). Think of lamps, hanging fixtures, and candles as accessories—something you can change with your mood and desire and match with your style. Experiment with light and lighting as you would with jewelry, shoes, and scarves when putting together an outfit. Remember how cool it looked when you paired that crazy leather jacket with a beaded top and jeans? The same principle can apply to lighting: Try hanging an elaborate chandelier with tiny, leopard fabric-covered shades in an ultramodern room. Or use simple, clear-glass cylinder lamps in a more traditional, Victorian setting.

While the right lighting can create an enchanting atmosphere, there's nothing remotely magical about electricity. Electricity is a wonderful thing; without it, our lives would be dark in the most literal sense. How does it work? Electrical current comes into your house through wires and leaves through wires. The current that flows along those "hot" wires is pressurized. That pressure is called *voltage*. Naturally, large electrical wires carry more current than small wires because their volume is greater. The current-carrying capacity of wires is called *amperage*, or *amps*. Access to electricity comes through receptacles, switches, and fixtures.

Electricity's first stop, however, is at your home's service panel, which is where circuit breakers or fuses (depending on the house) are located. It's essential that you get to know your service panel, which usually looks like a metal cabinet with a door. Why? Because sometimes a circuit overloads and can "trip," causing some of the power in your house to go out. There is usually no need to call an electrician or the super to restore a tripped circuit. It's an easy fix *if* you're familiar with your service panel.

DEFINING MOMENT

AMPERE (OR AMP): The rate at which electricity flows to a light, tool, or appliance.

ARMORED CABLE: Two or more wires grouped together and protected by a flexible metal tube.

CABLE: Two or more wires that are grouped together and protected by a covering.

CIRCUIT: A continuous loop of electrical current flowing along wires or cables.

CIRCUIT BREAKER: This safety device interrupts an electrical circuit in the event of an overload or short circuit.

CONDUCTOR: Any material that allows electrical current to flow through it, such as copper.

CONDUIT: A metal or plastic tube used to protect wires.

CURRENT: The movement of electrons along a conductor.

FEED WIRE: A conductor that carries 120-volt current uninterrupted from the service panel.

FUSE: A safety device, usually found in older homes, that interrupts electrical circuits during an overload or short circuit.

GROUNDING WIRE: Used in an electrical circuit to conduct current to the earth in the event of a short circuit, the grounding wire is usually a bare copper wire.

HOT WIRE: A wire that carries voltage; in an electrical circuit, the hot wire usually is covered with black or red insulation.

INSULATOR: A material, such as plastic or rubber, that resists the flow of electrical current. Insulating materials protect wires and cables.

OVERLOAD: A demand for more current than the circuit wires or electrical device was designed to carry, which usually causes a fuse to blow or a circuit breaker to trip.

POLARIZED RECEPTACLE: A receptacle designed to keep hot current flowing along black or red wires and neutral current flowing along white or gray wires.

RECEPTACLE: A device that provides plug-in access to electrical power.

SCREW TERMINAL: A place where a wire connects to a receptacle, switch, or fixture.

SERVICE PANEL: A metal box usually near the site where electrical power enters the house. The service panel has circuit breakers or fuses to protect each circuit.

SHORT CIRCUIT: An accidental and improper contact between two current-carrying wires, or between a current-carrying wire and a grounding conductor.

SWITCH: This device controls electrical current passing through hot circuit wires and is used to turn lights and appliances on and off.

UL: An abbreviation for Underwriters Laboratories, an organization that tests electrical devices and manufactured products for safety.

VOLTAGE (OR VOLTS): A measurement of electricity in terms of pressure.

WATTAGE (OR WATT): A measurement of electrical power in terms of total energy consumed. Watts can be calculated by multiplying the voltage times the amps.

WIRE NUT: A device used to connect two or more wires together.

Knowing how to turn off the power in your house is important if you are going to embark on even the simplest, most straightforward electrical project. Remember: Electricity is very serious business. But that doesn't mean you have to avoid electrical projects; it just means that you have to fully understand and follow directions carefully before embarking on any lighting project. I also believe that if you are embarking on complicated electrical projects such as rewiring your house, adding new wiring, or installing new fixtures where wiring does not already exist, you should hire a reputable licensed electrician.

You can't light up your life without some simple how-to information, so let me turn you on to some!

BRIGHT IDEAS

Simple measures can keep your lighting bright and your family safe.

- Make sure all lamps and light fixtures have the proper wattage bulb installed. A higher-than-indicated bulb can cause a blowout or, worse, an electrical fire. Lower wattage bulbs can be used safely. Example: Don't put a 100-watt bulb in a lamp that calls for a 75-watt bulb, but a 60-watt bulb is fine.
- Do not use extension cords as permanent wiring. If you need more outlets, consider having them installed by a licensed professional. Extension cords are for temporary use only.
- Make sure lamp and equipment cords are not draped over furniture or in areas where they could become tripping hazards.
- If you have small children, make sure every unused outlet is covered with a safety cap.

Mapping It Out
Create a Circuit or Fuse Map
Time: 30 minutes to 2 hours, depending on the size of your home

Having your circuits (or fuses) identified will help you cut power to specific areas of your house. It will also help you more quickly identify which circuit has been tripped if you lose power. Creating a good circuit map is time-consuming but easy. Having a friend help you will make the time go faster.

Always remember: Water conducts electricity. Do not embark on this project if the floor near the service panel is wet. Never stand in water (not even a drop!) when working with electricity.

What You Need
A friend (optional)
White masking tape
Indelible ink pen

How to Get It Done
1. Turn off all computers and ceiling fans. Leave on lights, radios, and TVs to help identify which switches or fuses turn off power in what rooms. This is especially helpful if you are working by yourself. When the music stops or the lights go out in a room, you know that switch or fuse controls those outlets.
2. Locate and open the service panel.
3. Using one hand (keep the other at your side) and starting at the top of the box, switch each circuit breaker to the off position. Have your friend tell you what lights (and related appliances) went out. Turn the switch back on.
4. Write the name of the room and any appliances on the white masking tape and number it.
5. Write that number on another piece of tape and attach it next to the appropriate circuit.
6. Attach the descriptive tape to the inside of the door so it corresponds to the correct switch. Many service panels have a map you can write on already attached to the door. If that's the case, use it instead of the tape for identifying notes.
7. Repeat this process until every circuit is identified.

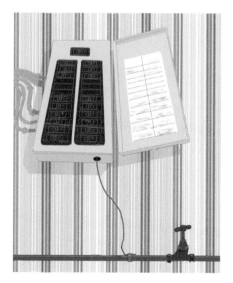

Get to know your circuit box and mark what each circuit breaker controls in your home.

Light Magic

Lighting is an extremely important element in decorating. We often choose a light fixture or lamp simply because it's pretty or because we think it will get the job done. In the process, we forget about its lighting capabilities or how it will blend and accent our décor. Selecting lamps that provide a particular kind of glow *and* that complement the style of a room can pull a look together while imparting plenty of practicality and attitude.

When you have more than one source of light in a room, you can change the mood with the flip of a switch. For example, when I entertain a special date at home, I like to turn off the overhead lights and turn on a few well-placed lamps to create a relaxing (and flattering) ambiance in my living room. Even the choice of bulbs can change the way a room looks: Adding low-wattage bulbs (25 or 40 watts, for example) to some of the lamps in a room lets you create a romantic mood. Pink or peach bulbs are especially flattering in a bedroom or bathroom. Full-spectrum bulbs are fantastic in reading lamps because the glow they cast is true to natural light without the glare, and therefore they are easy on the eyes.

Lighting serves three basic roles: general, task, and decorative or accent. All rooms benefit by using a combination of lighting types. Here's how.

General lighting gives overall background lighting, closely approximating natural daylight. It's glare-free light that bounces off walls and ceilings. Examples of general lighting fixtures include high hats, track lights, and hanging fixtures. When a dimmer control is installed on a general lighting switch, it can transform the general lighting into accent lighting by allowing you to lower the level of light to a soft glow.

Task lighting provides light where you need it to complete a specific job such as reading, cooking, putting on makeup, or working on the computer. Examples include reading lights, spotlights, under-the-counter lighting, and bathroom mirror lamps.

Accent or decorative lights add a bit of shimmer and color to a room without really lighting in a practical sense. Accent lights include sconces, colored lanterns, electric candles, uplight cans, picture lamps (narrow lamps attached to the top of artwork), or even a natural glow in the form of candles or a crackling blaze in the fireplace.

A living room should have good general lighting, task lights near chairs and sofas, and accent lights placed around the room on side tables, consoles, or even among a grouping of plants or over artwork. In my living room, I have good over-head light, but I also have an assortment of colored lanterns hanging from the ceiling and placed on side tables. Reading lamps are placed near comfortable chairs. So whether I'm reading a book or playing a game with Zachary, entertaining friends, or just relaxing after a long workweek, my choice of lighting can be controlled to make the room feel right.

Adult bedrooms, guest rooms, dressing rooms, and walk-in closets also need the right lighting for reading, getting dressed, and applying makeup. General lighting should be bright but soft and relaxing. Sconces and accent lamps can add glimmer and romance at the flip of a switch. Bedside lighting should also be bright enough if you want to curl up with a good book. Place dressing table lights on either side of the mirror rather than over it to lend an all-over glow instead of a harsh down light, which creates false shadows on the face. A good desk lamp is essential if you're plan-ning on doing work or writing in your bedroom.

Children's bedrooms need great general lighting for playtime. Older children will also need a good desk lamp for doing homework and craft projects. And in my expe-rience, every child needs a nightlight to protect from scary monsters under the bed and to light the way for late-night trips to the bathroom. You may be better off with overhead and wall fixtures in young children's rooms. Lamps can be toppled over and broken during rambunctious play.

Dining room lighting should be bright enough to see what you and your guests are eating, but not so bright that the bulbs are keeping the food hot! An overhead chandelier, pendant light, or other hanging fixture that can be dimmed is classic. Lamps flanking a sideboard or bar are also nice and are especially useful if you en-tertain and serve food buffet-style.

Bathroom lighting should be flattering and bright. You should be able to see what you're doing when you are getting yourself and your family ready for a busy day. Safety is an issue here, of course. But you should also be able to have soft light for long soaks in the tub. A dimmer is a good solution if you only have room for general lighting in a small bathroom—or any room for that matter.

Dim Some
Installing a Dimmer
Time: About 45 minutes

Installing a dimmer switch gives you so much more flexibility in a room. Dimmer switches come in do-it-yourself kits these days and are available at most department stores and home centers.

What You Need

Screwdriver
Dimmer switch kit
Wire cutter
Wire strippers
Pliers
2 wire nuts
Electrical tape

How to Get It Done

1. Turn off the circuit that you will be working on. Find the right breaker in the breaker box, and flip it to the "off" position. If you have a fuse box, find the right fuse and remove it completely from the panel. Double-check to make sure that the circuit is off by turning the light on. If the light doesn't go on, you've selected the right breaker or fuse.
2. Use a screwdriver to remove the switch plate.
3. Remove the switch from the workbox by unscrewing the screws on the top and bottom of the switch.
4. Disconnect the wires that are connected to the light switch by unscrewing the nut that connects them and separating them.
5. In dimmer kits, the wires have generally already been stripped back. If they are not, using a wire cutter, cut off the bare wire just below the plastic insulation on all three wires. Then use wire strippers to strip off about ⅜ inch of the insulation. This gives you a clean piece of wire for the new connection to the dimmer. If needed, strip the wires that are already attached to the dimmer switch.

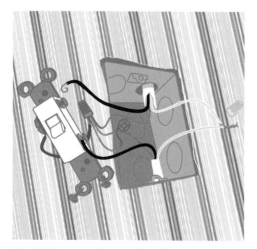

Step 4. Disconnect the wires from the old light switch.

6. Connect one of the black wires in the workbox to one from the dimmer switch by placing the bare wires next to each other. Then twist the wires in a clockwise direction with a pair of pliers, and finally twist on a wire nut. Make sure that the bare wires are completely encased in the wire nut. Do the same for the other set of black wires as well as the ground wires. Wrap electrical tape around the nut to meet the wires.

7. Bend the wires in a zigzag pattern so that they easily fold into the workbox. Push the switch into place. Adjust the switch so that it is perpendicular to the floor. Tighten the two screws that hold it in position in the workbox.

8. Install the new dimmer switch plate over the dimmer switch.

9. Switch the breaker back on (or reinstall the fuse). Test the dimmer to make sure your installation was successful. If the dimmer doesn't work, turn off the breaker and double-check your wiring connections.

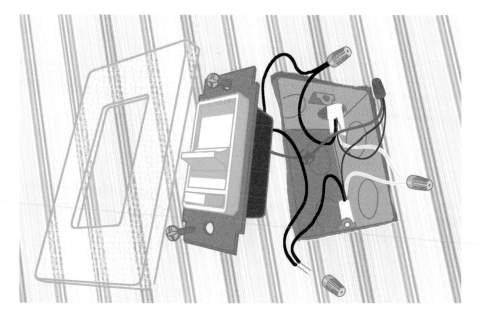

Step 6. Make sure bare wires are encased in wire nuts.

Shed New Light on the Subject!
Replace a Light Fixture
Time: About 45 minutes

Look for lighting inspiration whenever you are shopping—at a flea market, estate sale, junk shop, or even when you travel. You might find beautiful sconces or a chandelier and decide to redo a room around them. I added two hanging cone sconces on either side of my bed that I thought were truly eye-catching. Once they were in place, the whole feel of the room changed dramatically: It became slightly exotic and very soothing. So if you have hanging fixtures or wall sconces that are either out-of-date or clash with your new décor, it's easy to change them. This is a fairly simple procedure because the work of hardwiring behind the walls or in the ceiling has already been done.

Occasionally you will find an extra wire in the fixture's junction box (the box in the wall, right behind the fixture), which is generally red and usually referred to as a "neutral wire." If you find this to be the case in your box, I suggest that you consult a professional to find out how to address it. You don't have to hire an electrician. An associate in the electrical department of a home store can help you with this.

If there are only two wires in the box, here's how to change the fixture.

What You Need
Screwdriver

Replacement fixture

2 wire nuts

Wire strippers

How to Get It Done
1. Turn off the circuit that you will be working on. Find the right breaker in the breaker box and flip it to the "off" position. If you have a fuse box, find the right fuse, and remove it completely from the panel. You can verify that the correct circuit has been turned off if the light controlled by the switch no longer works. Or you can use a receptacle tester.
2. Remove the fixture by unscrewing the cover.

Step 3. Remove the old fixture.

Step 5. Connect the new wires to the house wires with wire nuts and twist.

Step 6. Attach the new fixture to the mounting strap.

3. Remove the fixture from the wires. The old fixture will have one white wire and one black wire, or a white wire with black tape at the end. If it has a third wire, as described on page 139, consult an electrical professional on how to proceed.

4. If there is a bare or green "ground" wire in the junction box (this is the box behind the fixture that holds it in place), unscrew it from the box, and install it under the green screw of the mounting box.

5. Splice the new fixture's wires to the house wires—black to black and white to white—using wire nuts. To splice, trim the insulation of the individual wires back about ¾ inch with a pair of wire strippers. Place the bare tips of the wires together, insert the wire nut, and turn it clockwise.

6. Tuck the wires into the box. Fasten the new fixture with the screws into the threaded holes in the mounting strap.

7. Attach the new fixture to the wall.

8. Install the lightbulb, turn on the power at the service panel, and check the fixture. Voila! You have a new light!

Note: If the new fixture's base is smaller than the old one, you may have to patch the wall. See "Patch Small, Medium, and Large Holes" on page 42 for instructions on patching. Be sure to tape off the new fixture to protect its surface while working with patch material.

Step 7. Attach the new fixture to the wall.

BASIC BLACKOUT KIT

Ice and snowstorms, hurricanes, and other severe weather can cause power outages. Even overuse of air-conditioners during a steamy heat wave can overload circuits and cause severe black- and brownouts. Having lived through the blackout of 2003, I know firsthand how scary a massive power outage can be, especially when you have young children. But if you're prepared, you can get through a few hours (or even a day or two) of powerlessness with minimal stress. A blackout kit, some well-positioned flashlights, and a sense of humor will see you through.

Store your blackout kit in an accessible place, such as the bottom of your pantry or hall closet, and make sure that everyone in your house knows where it is. Keep a flashlight with working batteries (test every few months and replace if necessary) in every bedside drawer, in specially designated places in the kitchen and living room, and, if you have a basement, at the top of your cellar stairs.

Here's a list of blackout kit essentials:
- $20 to $50 cash for any supplies you may need
- Battery-powered smoke alarm
- Candles in tall glass containers (you can buy these at the grocery store for a couple of dollars; *do not leave burning candles unattended!*)
- Drinking water, 4 gallon bottles for each family member
- First aid kit
- Flashlights with spare, fresh batteries
- Landline telephone (cordless phones do not work during blackouts)
- 3 days' worth of nonperishable food (replace it every year)
- Portable or transistor radio with extra batteries
- Blankets

Optional but helpful:
- "Blackout" teddy bear or other special stuffed animal (If you have little ones, a specially designated soft toy they can cuddle will comfort them)
- Deck of cards (there's nothing like candlelight poker to keep your mind off the darkness)

Re-Wired
Rewire a Lamp
Time: Less than 1 hour

BARBARA'S BEST-KEPT SECRET

Lamp wire comes in a variety of colors—silver, gold, clear, brown, white, and black—to name a few. Be sure to select the right wire for your lamp and décor. For example, clear glass lamps are best wired with clear wire.

After I changed my sconces, more lighting inspiration followed. I found some beautiful lamps in an antique shop. They're very decorative punched tin with colored glass inserts. I knew that they would make beautiful mood lighting, but the wiring was old and frayed. It's not hard to rewire an old lamp or make a lantern into a lamp, and it's very inexpensive, too. Most of the materials can be found in a home center or hardware store, and they will cost less than $10. In general, I think it's a good idea to rewire vintage lamps because you never know how old the wiring really is.

What You Need

Lamp with old wiring

Phillips head screwdriver with small head

Flat head screwdriver

Wire strippers

8-foot length electrical cord for lamps

Two-pole lamp socket

Two-pole plug

How to Get It Done

1. Unplug and remove the bulb if necessary from the lamp. Loosen the screw at the bottom of the socket shell with a screwdriver. It holds the shell to the rod in the lamp base. Using a flat head screwdriver, apply pressure to the shell where the word "press" is engraved to release the socket from the shell.
2. Pull the socket straight up, remove the cover, and use the small screwdriver to loosen the screws inside. Pull out the wires.
3. Slip the shell off of the rod. Pull the old electrical cord wire down through the bottom of the lamp base and discard.
4. Use wire strippers to remove about 1 inch of plastic covering from each end of an 8-foot length of electrical cord.
5. Thread the new cord up through the lamp base, and pull 3 inches up through the new shell and new socket.
6. Set the new shell onto the rod in the base of the lamp. Place the socket into the new shell, and push it down until you hear it click. Tighten the screw at bottom of the shell to hold it steady to the rod.

Step 2. Remove old wiring from the screws on the socket.

7. Separate the two wires of the cord. You can pull them apart with your hands. Wind each side of the stripped wire clockwise around the screws on either side of the socket. Tighten the screws with a screwdriver.

8. In vintage lamps, you often have to remove the screws holding the plastic cover to the plug, and slip off the cover. Thread the bottom of the cord through the cover and the new plug, and separate the wires. Next, tie what is called an underwriter's knot at the end of the cord. This will prevent it from being pulled back through the lamp rod. To make the knot, hold the separated wires out like a Y. Make a loop on each end of the wire, holding the end of one loop in front of the joined cord and the end of the other loop at the back of the joined cord. Then, slip each end through the loop formed by the opposite wire and then pull to tighten the knot. Pull on the plug end of the cord so the knot fits snugly against the socket cap. Twist the wire, clockwise, around the screws on either side of the plug, and tighten the screws with the screwdriver. Snap the cover over the plug, and then tighten the cover screws until firmly in place.

9. Test the lamp by screwing the bulb into the socket and plugging in the lamp.

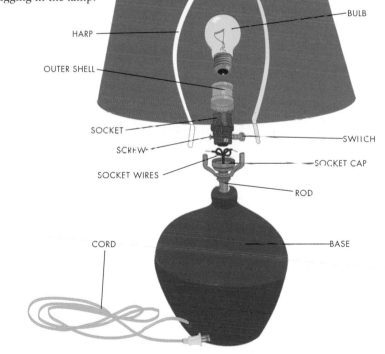

Step 8. Create what's called an underwriter's knot with the wires before attaching them to the screws.

SHADE

BULB

HARP

OUTER SHELL

SOCKET

SCREW

SOCKET WIRES

SWITCH

SOCKET CAP

ROD

CORD

BASE

Before: My old lantern was nice, but not spectacular.

An Illuminating Switch

New life can be given to any lanternlike hanging fixture, without any rewiring at all, simply by changing its housing. I had a very plain lantern fixture in my entryway. It was nice, but I knew it could be better. I found another large lantern (similar to the small ones I transformed into electrified lamps) that I knew would fit over the old lantern's housing. My hanging fixture is quite large, so I needed four friends to help me unscrew it from the top cap. Once we got it down, we all worked together to screw the new lantern onto the old cap. If your hanging lantern fixture is not as large as mine, you can probably do this on your own. However, I recommend having a friend along no matter what the size of your light because you will be on a ladder. It's best to have someone on the ground when you are working at a height.

Even if you don't have a lantern fixture like mine, the idea of transforming something you already have is what I want you to think about. Lamps and lighting fixtures can be changed with paint, fabric, and a little imagination. Simply switching a lampshade can change the look of a lamp. Covering a shade with fabric, painting a lamp base with new color, or even covering it with mosaic pieces gives you a whole new lamp! Chandeliers can be enhanced by adding crystals and beads or can be simplified by taking them off. The message is to look at what you have and think about how you can change and improve it. And then go ahead and do it! Light up your life!

Now that everything in your home is appropriately lighted, let's make sure your plumbing is in good order. Stay with me . . . it's not so hard, and learning how to solve plumbing troubles will save you money (which you can spend on something truly beautiful).

After: A whole new light—no electrical work required!

Chapter 6
Plumbing the Depths

It's a fact: Plumbing problems always seem to stop us in our tracks. It's probably because we can't see a lot of what plumbing really *is*. Water and waste pipes are generally buried behind walls or under floors, and so what we can't see, we often don't understand. Many of us (men included) are a little scared of what goes on inside those pipes. But *you* don't have to be scared because plumbing isn't as intimidating as it seems. Once I understood what plumbing was all about, I found that it isn't a big deal. It's quite logical, in fact. Once you get a grip on the basics, you'll be able to make many repairs in your house that would otherwise cost you an arm and a leg if fixed by a plumber (who may not even show up!).

Why *not* do it yourself? You'll feel fantastic about getting rid of that irritating drip, that annoying and costly running toilet, and the constantly clogged kitchen drain.

Of all home improvement projects, the feeling of accomplishment and pride you will get from having successfully solved a plumbing problem will make you feel like a superhero. Indeed, you will be a megastar in the eyes of your family and friends! And it doesn't have to stop with quick clog fixes and repairing basic toilet trouble. You can actually update and add value to your home by learning the skills in this chapter and then combining them with many other how-to projects in this book. For example, I love the idea that you can fix and upgrade your bathroom and make it go from blah to spa in just a weekend or two. I want you to have the *best* bathroom on your block, and I want you to do a lot of it yourself.

So grab your wrench and come along with me. You don't even have to change your shoes. (I do my plumbing in high heels, and I do not care what anyone thinks!)

SAFETY NOTES

Remember to always follow manufacturer's instructions when using any product or tool, even if you've used it in the past. Follow manufacturer's recommended safety precautions when working with plumbing products. Manufacturers take a lot of time to write user-friendly instructions, and they know better than anyone about how to use their particular material or tool. Always work in a clear area. Go slowly and always have a bucket and rag nearby to catch leaks and draining water. A shop vac really comes in handy when dealing with plumbing projects: It sucks up both solid debris and water. It isn't very expensive and can often be purchased for less than $50. When working with new fixtures, such as a faucet or showerhead, remember to use a cloth or rag under the pliers so that you don't scratch the fittings. Finally, remember that water and electricity don't mix. *Never*, under any circumstances, turn on light if you are standing in water because it will cause electrical shock.

That Sinking Feeling

Is there anything more irritating than a dripping faucet or a sink that won't drain properly? What about those corroded 1970s fixtures staring you in the face every morning? That's not the best way to wake up! We have so much to do during the day that we should all be able to start the day as peacefully and beautifully as possible. It doesn't matter if you love to luxuriate in the bathroom or you prefer to be in and out in a matter of minutes. Having a sink and faucet that work well helps you get the right start to what will most likely be a hectic day. Even the kitchen sink plays an important part in a smoothly running day: It's no fun to prepare a quick cup of coffee or boil water for a pasta supper if the sink is acting up!

Here are some simple solutions to getting your bathroom and kitchen sinks quiet, clear, and looking gorgeous!

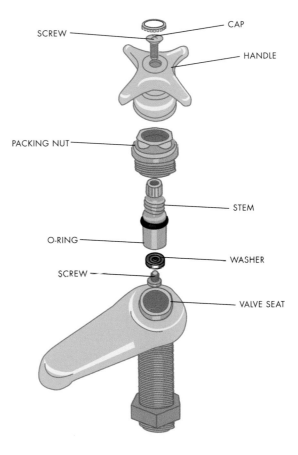

SCREW — CAP

HANDLE

PACKING NUT

STEM

O-RING

WASHER

SCREW —

VALVE SEAT

Fixing a leaky faucet is a do-it-yourself job you can easily handle.

The Big Drip Faucet Fix
Repair a Dripping Faucet
Time: About 30 minutes

A dripping faucet is an annoying reminder that you're wasting water and literally throwing it and your hard-earned dollars down the drain. Old-fashioned compression faucets cause most leaks. Modern faucets are washerless and virtually dripless. Simply replacing an old-fashioned faucet's O-ring or the washer can usually stop a drip coming from the spout or handle.

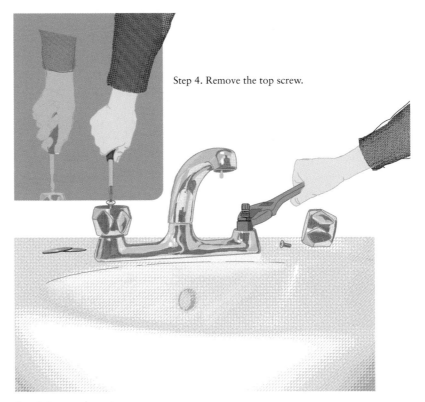

Step 4. Remove the top screw.

Step 5. Loosen the nut.

What You Need

Plastic wrap
Terry-cloth towel
Flat head screwdriver
Phillips head screwdriver
8-inch adjustable wrench or 6-inch slip joint pliers
Washer (if it needs to be replaced)
O-ring(s) (if they need to be replaced)
Utility knife
Heat-resistant lubricant

How to Get It Done

1. Shut off the water at the local shut-off valve located under the sink. Get rid of any water left by turning the handles and letting the water drain out. You can also test to make sure you actually turned off the water supply this way.
2. Place a folded piece of plastic wrap over the drain and then cover it and the sink with a terry-cloth towel. These two layers will protect the sink and stop any small bits from falling down the drain.
3. If there's a cap on the handle, gently pry it off with a flat head screwdriver.
4. Using a Phillips head screwdriver, take off the screw that holds the dripping handle in place.
5. Using your wrench or pliers, loosen the nut that holds the stem. Once you have it off, remove the stem.
6. First check the washer. It's the little disc screwed to the bottom of the stem. If it's cracked or seems brittle, replace it. Take it to the hardware store and find a matching one for pennies.
7. Now check the O-ring. It's like a little rubber band that circles the stem. There might be more than one. If any of them look broken or otherwise damaged, cut them off with a utility knife.
8. Replace the O-rings with matching ones from the hardware store. It's a good idea to coat the stem with a bit of heat-resistant lubricant first. You can use the flat head screwdriver to help guide the O-rings into place.
9. Now reassemble the faucet by reversing the direction of steps 3 to 5.
10. Remove the towel and plastic wrap and turn the shut-off valve back on.

Step 6. Inspect the washer and replace it if it's damaged.

Step 7. Inspect the O-ring and replace it if it's damaged.

Top It Off!
Replace a Top-Mounted Faucet
Time: About 45 minutes

Once you've become expert at cleaning out clogs and unstuffing sinks, you may want to treat yourself and your bathroom to a brand-new faucet. A new fixture, available in any number of finishes, from shining chrome to brushed nickel, might be just the "jewelry" your bathroom or kitchen needs. Sometimes just changing this fixture is enough to update a drab bathroom or kitchen. Plus, replacing an old faucet with a new "washerless" model will eliminate drips and leaks.

Consider this: A new faucet, some fresh paint on the walls and cabinets, a new shower curtain, and coordinating towels are easy but effective ways to upgrade and modernize your bathroom, without spending big bucks on a serious renovation.

What You Need
> 8-inch adjustable wrench or 6-inch slip joint pliers
> Towel
> Penetrating oil lubricant
> 50–50 solution of vinegar and water
> Scouring pad
> Clean rags
> Plumber's putty or silicone caulk (if your new faucet does not have
>   a rubber or plastic gasket for the base)
> Faucet replacement set

How to Get It Done
1. Using an adjustable wrench or slip joint pliers, turn off the two shut-off valves under the faucet you're replacing. Then open the faucet and allow it to drain and release any pressure.
2. Disconnect the water supply lines from the faucet only.
3. Line the sink with a towel to protect it.
4. Remove the old faucet from the sink. It's held in place by nuts located underneath the sink, so you're going to have to go down under the sink to loosen the nuts with pliers or a wrench. If it's a very old fixture and the nuts are rusted or

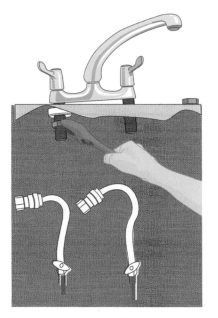

Step 4. Detach the faucet from the sink.

corroded, apply penetrating oil lubricant and allow it to sit and work according to the manufacturer's instructions before trying to remove the nuts.

5. Once the faucet has been removed, you'll most likely see a lot of gunk in the area where the faucet was attached. Clean it off before installing the new faucet. A 50-50 solution of vinegar and water will help dissolve the buildup. Work it in with a scouring pad, rinse, and dry off the area with a clean rag.

6. If your new faucet does not have a rubber or plastic gasket for the base, you can go ahead and install the faucet, but you will need to run a bead of plumber's putty or silicone caulk around the faucet base.

7. Put the new faucet in place, pressing against the putty to assure a good seal if necessary.

8. Get back under the sink and install the washers and mounting nuts on the tail-pieces. Tighten the nuts by hand.

9. Align the faucet with the back of the sink and tighten the mounting nuts with pliers or a wrench. If necessary, use another clean rag to wipe away excess putty from around the base.

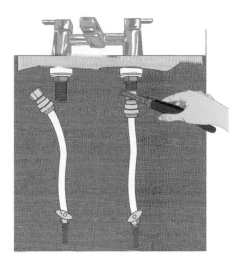

Step 10. Reattach the supply lines under the sink.

10. Hook up the supply lines. If you are replacing a faucet that comes with a sprayer, don't turn the water back on until you install that.

11. Run a bead of plumber's putty to the base of the sprayer holder, if the sprayer base does not come with a rubber or plastic gasket. Insert the holder into the hole and tighten it in place with the mounting nut. Wipe away any excess plumber's putty from around the base of the holder.

12. Insert the supply tube of the sprayer through the holder from the top. The sprayer will sit in place in the holder.

13. Get back under the sink and screw the sprayer supply hose to the hose nipple on the bottom of the faucet. Tighten the nut with a wrench or water pump pliers.

14. Turn on the water and test the faucet and sprayer.

Note: If your faucet comes with a pop-up drain assembly, follow the step-by-step instructions included with your faucet kit to install it.

Clog Stopper
Clean and Adjust a Pop-Up Sink Drain Stopper
Time: About 30 minutes

A stopped-up sink is often caused by the stuff that collects in the pop-up drain stopper (most often hair, toothpaste, soap, and dental floss). You can get rid of the buildup in just a few minutes. It's good maintenance to clean the drain stopper whenever you think the water is draining out of the sink more slowly than it should. Allowing buildup to accumulate month after month can cause bigger clogs that are harder to clean out. The seconds you take while using the sink will save cleaning time later on.

What You Need

Pliers
Rubber gloves
Small bottlebrush or old toothbrush

How to Get It Done

1. Raise the stopper lever to the full upright (closed) position.
2. Use pliers or your hand to unscrew the nut that holds the pivot rod to the sink drain.
3. Pull the pivot rod out of the drainpipe to release the stopper.
4. Remove the stopper. Clean the debris from the stopper with your hands (wear rubber gloves if you like) and a small bottlebrush or old toothbrush.
5. Reinstall the stopper.

Tako the Plunge
Clear a Clogged Sink Drain
Time: About 15 minutes

I have a lot of friends who have children Zachary's age. All of us moms love doing things in the kitchen with our kids—from melting butter for microwave popcorn to making craft projects (think glue and glitter!). At one time or another each of us has faced a clogged sink, usually after an afternoon of cooking something up in the kitchen. Luckily, kitchen sink clogs can be undone quickly.

Unclogging bathroom drains seems like a constant activity in one friend's house. She has two teenage girls with lots of hair products and makeup. And a lot of it is trying to get down the drain. It usually doesn't make it all the way down, which is why I recommended the following technique to my friend.

What You Need

Rag

Plunger

How to Get It Done

1. Remove the drain stopper. You may have to remove the pivot rod to free the stopper. (See instructions in "Clean and Adjust a Pop-Up Sink Drain Stopper" on the opposite page.) Some pop-up stoppers lift out directly and others turn counterclockwise. If it's a kitchen sink, remove the strainer.
2. If you are clearing a bathroom sink, stuff a wet rag in the sink overflow opening to prevent air from breaking the suction of the plunger. The overflow is the opening located in the sink under the faucet area or opposite it. If you are clearing a double kitchen sink, remove the strainer and stuff a wet rag in the drain of the other, clog-free sink.
3. Place the plunger cup over the drain and run enough water to cover the lip of the cup. Use the handle to move the center of the cup up and down rapidly and forcefully without breaking the seal of the plunger lip.
4. Reinstall the stopper.

Trap It
Remove and Clean a Sink Drain Trap
Time: About 30 minutes

If cleaning the pop-up stopper and plunging doesn't get rid of the clog, you may have to clean out the sink trap. That's the U-shaped pipe below the sink. Cleaning it out seems pretty daunting, especially because it requires loosening and temporarily removing the trap so it can be emptied of the buildup that is obstructing the water, but it's a straightforward fix. It's also a job that a plumber will charge big bucks for, so why not learn to do yourself? With the money you save, go ahead and treat yourself to something nice. You deserve it for being such a plumbing genius.

What You Need
Bucket
Pliers or pipe wrench
Small bottlebrush or old toothbrush

How to Get It Done
1. Place a bucket under the trap to catch water and waste material.
2. Loosen the slip nuts on the trap bend with pliers or a pipe wrench. Then unscrew the nuts by hand, slide them away from the connections, and carefully pull off the trap bend.
3. Dump out waste material and clean the trap with a small bottlebrush or old toothbrush. Inspect the slip-nut washers for wear and replace them, if necessary.
4. Reinstall the trap and tighten the slip nuts. Don't overtighten or you could strip the nuts. Test the drain by running water. If it leaks, tighten the slip nuts another quarter-turn.

Feeling Flush

Have you ever flushed the toilet, expecting the water to go down the drain and instead it just sits there or worse travels up and over the rim and puddles on the floor? This nightmare scenario is played out all too often in homes. Clogged, running, and leaky toilets seem to be more anxiety-producing than any other plumbing problem.

Understanding what happens when you flush may help demystify fixing the toilet when it doesn't. It's pretty simple, actually. First, as you push down the handle, the chain or lift arm inside the tank lifts the flapper up. The water held in the tank flows through the flush valve opening into the toilet's bowl. The water from the tank forces the wastewater in the bowl through the trap (the U-shaped area under the bowl) and

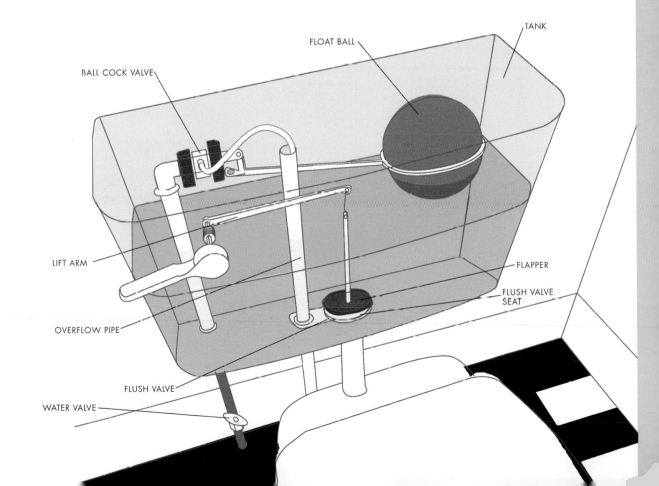

BALL COCK VALVE

FLOAT BALL

TANK

LIFT ARM

OVERFLOW PIPE

FLUSH VALVE

WATER VALVE

FLAPPER

FLUSH VALVE SEAT

into the main drain. Once the tank is empty, the flapper seals the tank and the ball cock refills it. When the tank is full, the float ball shuts off the ball cock valve.

A stuffed-up toilet can be the result of anything from small toys that were playfully flushed and have gotten stuck to carelessly discarded hair, which accumulates along the inside of the drainpipe and eventually causes a clog. Most of these annoying issues are easy to fix with a few specialized but inexpensive tools and some know-how.

DEFINING MOMENT

BALL COCK VALVE: Believe it or not, this is the water supply valve.

FLAPPER: This is a rubbery plug attached to the lift chain.

FLOAT BALL: This ball rides on the surface of the water in the tank. When the tank is full, the float ball shuts off the ball cock.

FLUSH VALVE: This is a connection that consists of the flapper and the flush valve seat.

FLUSH VALVE SEAT: This brass or plastic sealant ring is located at the bottom of the tank.

LIFT ARM: This thin metal rod inside the tank connects to the flush handle and raises the flapper valve.

MAIN DRAIN: The slanting pipe in the basement or crawl space that carries wastes to a sewer or septic tank.

MAIN WATER VALVE: Located on the wall near the floor, this is a knob you twist to turn the water supply on and off.

OVERFLOW PIPE: This is a long, hollow tube, fastened to the bottom of the tank.

TANK: The large ceramic container located behind the toilet bowl, the tank fills with and holds water for each flush.

TRAP: This is the U-shaped canal where wastewater goes as it leaves the toilet bowl.

Handle It!

Adjust a Toilet Handle

Time: About 15 minutes

A toilet handle can stick or loosen over time so that one day it just doesn't function at all. Both problems can be remedied in the same way.

What You Need

Bottlebrush or old toothbrush

Vinegar

Toilet tank chain, if necessary (a length of chain can be bought at a hardware store)

Long nose pliers

How to Get It Done

1. Remove the tank cover and check the mounting nut (located on the inside behind the handle) for lime buildup. This can prevent it from working. Clean the mounting nut with a bottlebrush or an old toothbrush dipped in vinegar. Test the handle to see if that does the trick.

2. If that doesn't work, check the chain that connects the lift arm to the flapper. There should be about ½ inch of slack in the chain. Adjust the slack by hooking the chain in a different hole in the handle or by removing the extra links with long nose pliers. If the chain is broken, replace it. You can buy this single part at a home center or hardware store.

Toilet Overboard!
Clear a Toilet Clog or Overflow
Time: About 20 minutes

There are few household problems as scary as an overflowing toilet. The first time I experienced this "event," I thought I would cry. There's a real feeling of helplessness when water starts pouring out over the rim of the toilet bowl all over the floor. Don't panic! There is a way to stop the overflow, which is generally caused by a clog in the drain.

What You Need
Flanged plunger
2-gallon bucket of water
Closet auger
Shop-Vac or bucket and mops

How to Get It Done
1. Place the cup of the flanged plunger over the drain outlet and plunge up and down rapidly while maintaining a seal around the lip of the cup.
2. Slowly pour a 2-gallon bucket of water into the bowl to clear the drain. Repeat plunging, if necessary.
3. If that doesn't work, an object may be obstructing the drain. A closet auger, sometimes called a toilet auger, will help. Push the auger cable into the trap until the bend sits in the drain opening. Crank the auger handle in a clockwise direction to break up the clog or snag obstructions. Continue to crank as you retrieve the cable and pull the obstruction out of the trap.
4. You may have quite a mess to clean up. That's where the Shop-Vac or bucket and mops will come in handy.
5. If more than one toilet or drain in your home is backing up, the point where the waste lines come together could be blocked. Long augers are available for these situations and are best used by a licensed plumber. Here's what the plumber will do: If the main drain line doesn't have a clean-out access, a long auger, or "snake," can be inserted directly through the toilet flange. This may require temporarily removing the toilet.

Run Away
Repair a Running Toilet
Time: About 20 minutes

A running toilet is a nuisance and a waste of water. Fortunately, it's also a home repair problem that can be solved quickly. There are a couple of things that can complicate this otherwise straightforward repair. If the toilet is not draining properly, don't flush until it begins to drain. As long as the toilet is otherwise working, stopping the water from running is simply a matter of finding and fixing the cause. One of these solutions should allow your tank to refill and stay full, which means no more wasted water.

What You Need
Float ball (if yours isn't working properly)
6-in-1 interchangeable screwdriver
Toilet repair kit

How to Get It Done
1. Remove the lid and check the lift arm or chain attached to the tank flapper to see if there is any problem with twisting, erosion, or buildup that is preventing the flapper from making a complete seal.
2. Lift the float ball up. If this stops the water from running, try bending the arm so the float ball is buoyant. If the float ball is not floating on top of the water, unscrew the old one and replace it with a new one from the toilet repair kit.
3. If the toilet continues to run, there may be buildup or some kind of sediment that is not allowing the stopper to close properly. Check the flush valve and the flush valve seat to see whether there is any damage. The flapper and the valve must be replaced if they are broken.

SAFETY NOTES

Be cautious when using any chemical drain openers. The chemicals that could unclog your drain can also damage the finish of your toilet. Chemical products may also damage septic systems so if you have one, check the label carefully before proceeding.

A New Seat for the Throne
Replace a Toilet Seat
Time: Less than 30 minutes

As I said earlier, a beautiful new faucet and some snazzy bathroom accessories can help create a spa-like atmosphere in any bathroom. Another simple fix—changing a toilet seat—completes your new look for very little money and effort. And sometimes a change of seat is all that's necessary to make a toilet look new.

Toilet seats are made in two standard shapes, rounded and elongated, and they are not interchangeable. You can tell by looking carefully at the old one but, to be sure, you can take the old one with you to the store and match it up.

What You Need
Wrench
Flat head screwdriver
Rags
New toilet seat

How to Get It Done
1. Remove the old seat by undoing the mounting-bolt-and-nut assemblies. Old-fashioned seats may have to be removed by reaching under the back of the bowl and using a wrench on the nuts. On modern seats (post 1960), the bolts are separate from the hinge. They are inserted through housings at each end of the hinge. Use a flat head screwdriver to pry the two covers open. Unscrew the bolts and lift the old seat off.
2. Most new seats will come with two foam-and-epoxy washers. They look like two squares of thick cardstock with a hole in the center of each. If your seat came with those pieces, turn the new seat upside down, peel the protective paper off each washer, and center them on the bottom of each bolt-head housing.
3. Turn the seat over, line up the holes, and bolt it to the bowl. With old-style seats, set washers on the bolts and run the nuts up snug, but not too tight. With new-style seats, start the nut on each bolt by reaching underneath. You should then be able to hand-tighten each bolt without holding the nut because they are usually self-holding. Close the housing covers and you're done!

Shower Power

A brisk shower is sometimes all I need to get me going—that and a big hug from Zach. I love taking long, hot showers after a tough day at work or on the weekends. A strong rush of water running down my back is so invigorating. Don't get me wrong, a long soak in the tub is wonderful, but a great shower is one of the few ways I can get energized *and* relaxed at the same time.

Are you renovating your bathroom or making decisions about a new house and one of the bathrooms is too small for a tub? Don't be disappointed. There are so many fashionable choices in showers today that a tub-less bathroom can be as luxurious and beautiful as any spa! In my bathroom, I chose a porcelain shower basin and beautiful etched glass for the door and surround. You don't have to settle for plain glass. Myriad choices in glass today make it possible to create a truly unique shower, and most decorative glass doesn't cost any more than standard glass.

I also chose a balance pressure valve for its expensive look (but not a high price tag). A balance pressure valve is made to look like an expensive thermostatic valve. A thermostatic valve is much more expensive (up to $1,000) because it gives both temperature control, as well as pressure/volume control, by using separate shut-off valves from the thermostat. But a standard balance pressure valve (often less than $200) exerts full water pressure with just hot and cold temperature regulation. You cannot control the volume or pressure of the water coming out. But manufacturers are making balance pressure valves that look like their expensive counterparts but cost hundreds of dollars less. A thermostatic valve is a luxury item and not necessary to take a great shower. But if you can get the look for less, why not do it?

A pressure valve is a small detail with great impact—and it's affordable, too.

A shower-only bathroom can be just as luxurious as one with a fancy bathtub.

OPPOSITE: Pretty etched glass brings shower style to a whole new level of beauty.

BARBARA'S BEST-KEPT SECRET

Keep your showerhead looking new by using a cloth under the pliers. This will protect the fittings when you remove and attach the showerhead. When removing the old showerhead, wrap the showerhead pipe stem with a piece of cloth or rag to protect the finish.

Off with Its Head!
Replace a Showerhead
Time: About 20 minutes

It's easy to make an old shower look new. Along with changing an old faucet and replacing a toilet seat, a new showerhead can perk up an old bathroom and even improve the strength of the shower flow. Why? Sometimes an old showerhead can get clogged or corroded and that can impact the flow of water through it. Besides, a bright new showerhead is such an effortless way to transform your bathroom, especially if you want to add a massage feature. While you're at it, get rid of drain clogs so that the shower water runs off quickly and doesn't stand in the basin. Make sure your shower floor is dry before starting this project to ensure that you don't slip. Wear sneakers or other flat rubber-soled shoes. No heels here!

What You Need
   8-inch slip joint pliers
   Teflon sealant tape
   Cloth rag
   New showerhead

How to Get It Done
1. Using the pliers, twist off the old showerhead (counterclockwise), while holding the shower pipe stem.
2. Wrap the Teflon sealant tape two or three times around the threads at the end of the pipe stem.
3. Using a cloth under the pliers to protect the new showerhead fitting, screw on the new showerhead (clockwise) until tight. Stand back, turn on the water, and test for leaks. You've earned that hot, steamy shower—you installed it yourself!

No Strain Drain
How to Clear a Shower Drain
Time: About 15 minutes

Keep in mind that a shower drain can clog just like a sink drain. If the water seems to be running out slowly after you shower, check to make sure the drain is clear. Hair and bits of soap are the biggest culprits, making clearing the drain a straightforward production.

What You Need

Flat head screwdriver
Flashlight
Stiff wire
Plunger
Hand auger

How to Get It Done

1. Check for clogs. Using a flat head screwdriver, remove the strainer cover on the drain. With a flashlight, look for hair clogs in the drain opening. Bend a hook end on a stiff wire and use it to pull hair and other obstructions from the drain.
2. Use a plunger to clear the clog. Place the rubber cup over the drain and run enough water into the shower to cover the lip of the cup. Work the handle up and down forcefully without breaking the seal of the lip.
3. More stubborn shower drain clogs can be cleared with a hand auger. Do not confuse a hand auger with a closet or toilet auger. They are two different tools and are not interchangeable.

I hope this chapter has proven to you that many plumbing issues can be addressed easily and simply. A little confidence and the right tools are really all you need. Next time there's a clog or a drip, promise me you'll tackle it on your own. And let me know how you did. I'm always interested and inspired by your efforts! In the meantime, let's get going on all small repairs and improvements you can make that will make your house and your life hum a happier tune.

Chapter 7

Smooth Operation: Fast Fixes, Everyday Upgrades, and Clutter Control

When the things around me work, my life works.

Staying on top of the details—making small improvements or minor repairs, doing regular maintenance, and controlling clutter—all add up to one thing: stress-free living. As I said in the beginning of this book, doorknobs that turn properly and kitchen knobs that don't fall off when you pull them make life a lot more pleasant. I almost don't go through a day without picking up a hammer or a screwdriver and doing something big or small, whether it's tightening the hinges on a door, hanging a basketball hoop for Zachary, or transforming a hallway closet into a new place to organize out-of-season clothes. Doing all these little things around the house is like second nature to me because I've learned that maintaining my environment makes my life better, easier, and more enjoyable. And I find that when I've made a small repair or completed a household improvement project, I feel as though a weight has been lifted off my shoulders. I think you know what I mean: It's one less thing to worry about, and it's one more thing to feel good about.

Many maintenance and repair jobs can be done in just a few minutes and transforming improvements can be accomplished in an hour or two, or in a weekend. That's a very small investment of time, and the payoff is huge.

SAFETY NOTES

Remember to always follow the manufacturer's instructions when using any product or tool, even if you've used it in the past. Manufacturers take a lot of time to write user-friendly instructions, and they know better than anyone about how to use their particular materials or tools. Also remember when embarking on any repair project to work in an area that has been cleared of debris, or any breakable or movable objects. When you are working with saws or other power tools, wear safety glasses and gloves. Follow product instructions. When working with paints or solvents of any kind, make sure the room is well ventilated. Wear a mask and safety glasses for protection against fumes and dust. Please dispose of solvents in a way that complies with local environmental rules.

For example, I recently changed the hardware on my kitchen cabinets. It was easy and fun, the bigger pulls make the cabinets function better, and the kitchen looks like it was completely redone! You'll see for yourself in this chapter.

Clutter is another obstacle that keeps us from getting things done. If we can't find our bills, we can't pay them. If our summer clothes are out of reach, we may end up buying new ones we don't really need or even want. If the dining room is filled with sports equipment, boxes of books, and discarded toys, how can we enjoy a family meal or sit quietly and write letters or do homework with our kids?

Broken furniture, drawers that stick, and claustrophobic clutter equals stress, plain and simple. Disorganized rooms and closets, dull cabinets, plain walls, and ugly furniture conspire against us to make us feel weary and uninspired. Getting organized and fixing what's broken is going to do so much for you and your family. Improving what you have and making it pretty and functional will give you and your home a new lease on life. That's what this chapter is all about: to help you see that little changes are not trivial at all, but rather, important and even monumental in the way they can make you feel.

The Big Fix

One way to ensure that you will keep up with repairs around the house is by having tools you love to use easily accessible. I keep my tool kit in the kitchen for easy access. For me, tools are accessories as important as a pair of fabulous shoes or a great-looking watch. I wouldn't be without them. In my experience, if tools are nearby, you're more prone to use them and much more likely to tackle small repair jobs when they crop up.

Problems happen in every room of the house. In this section, I'll show you how to fix and repair a variety of household problems that I find to be the most common and that friends and women in general have asked about most frequently, from chipped porcelain to wobbly ceiling fans to broken chairs. Sharing your know-how with your friends and family will give you an even bigger boost!

I took control of my clothes by redoing my closet. You'll see the end result later.

The Case of the Chipped Tub
Repair a Chipped Tub
Time: About 30 minutes, plus drying time

The phone company was repairing a friend's telephone line. He was examining the phone box, which happened to be located in a bathroom in the back of her old Victorian house. The repairman accidentally dropped his pliers on the corner of my friend's newly installed porcelain tub—and *whack*—the force of the tool chipped its edge. What to do?

No need to rip out the tub and replace it with another new one. (What kind of a nightmare would *that* be?) With a steady hand and a few simple items, I helped my friend repair the chip, and before long she was enjoying a long, hot soak. You can use this simple fix to repair a chip in any porcelain or fiberglass tub, sink, or toilet. I have even filled in cracks in porcelain tiles with this technique. Mixing enamel paint with white repair compound allows you to more closely match unusual colors, too. Porcelain or fiberglass chips can be sharp, so put on rubber gloves before you begin work on this project.

What You Need
Rubber gloves
Medium sandpaper or an emery board
Clean cloths
Rubbing alcohol
Wooden skewer
Porcelain or fiberglass repair compound
Enamel hobby paint (½- and ¼-ounce jars are available at art supply stores and
   hobby shops)
Scrap glass or tile
Single-edged razor blade
Cotton swabs
Fingernail polish remover

How to Get It Done

1. Put on rubber gloves. Sand the damaged area with medium sandpaper or an emery board until the edges of the chip are smooth. Take care not to sand any area other than the chipped portion because the sandpaper will scratch the porcelain.

2. Clean the chipped spot using a cloth dampened with rubbing alcohol. Wait for the alcohol to dry completely before applying the repair material.

3. Use the wooden skewer to mix the repair compound with the enamel hobby paint on a clean piece of scrap glass or tile until it matches your porcelain. Add a little compound at a time. Start over again if it's not a good match.

4. Scoop a little of the compound onto a single-edged razor blade and apply it to the damaged area. Be careful with the blade! Build up the chip by starting in the center and working out to the edges and overlapping the outline of the chip. Scrape off excess until the compound lies flush with the surface of the surrounding area.

5. After the patch dries (according to compound manufacturer's instructions), use a cotton swab saturated with fingernail polish remover to remove excess repair compound and blend the edges of the repair compound into the porcelain. Allow the repair to dry overnight.

A porcelain or fiberglass repair kit and some hobby paint allows you to make a virtually invisible repair.

Fan Club
Repair a Noisy, Shaky Fan
Time: About 45 minutes

I get so many e-mails asking about how to fix a wobbly fan that sometimes I think the entire country is shaking! It's not surprising, though, because ceiling fans are such a great, low-energy way to cool your home. A lot of people have them. Luckily, you can fix the problem easily in a few simple steps.

If you think that the fan problem is a loose screw near the electrical box (located in the ceiling right above the fan's motor), make sure to turn off the electricity at the service panel before proceeding.

What You Need
Phillips head screwdriver
Tape measure
Pliers

How to Get It Done
1. Check the fan blades to see if they are loose. If your fan is installed from the ceiling by a rod that extends down from the electrical box to the motor, check the connection between the rod and the motor and tighten any and all loose screws with a screwdriver or pair of pliers.
2. If the ceiling motor is attached directly to the ceiling, examine the ceiling mounting and tighten any and all loose screws.
3. Measure the distance of the blades from the ceiling. It is important that all the blades reside on the same plane. Hold one end of the measuring tape at the ceiling while rotating the blades manually to check the distance.
4. If a blade is not level or an equal distance to the other blades, you must gently bend the blade that is out of place. It is easier to do this step with an extra pair of hands. One person should hold the fan while the other person bends the blade.

Top Drawer
Free a Stubborn Drawer
Time: 10 to 15 minutes

Okay, now that the ceiling fan in your bedroom is turning quietly, you can get dressed in peace. Except that . . . you can't get your sock drawer to open with ease! I understand your frustration. My house is near the water, and that means the ever-changing humidity levels and weather conditions constantly affect the wood in my house, making it expand and contract. Doors stick and even floorboards shift slightly. The most annoying occurrence by far, though, is how the wooden drawers in dressers and in the kitchen get stuck when they expand. As a result, I sometimes find myself fighting to get them to open.

There are a couple of simple ways to get unstuck. If you absolutely cannot get the drawer out at all, you may have to wait until cooler weather to try the following fixes. The cooler weather will help the wood contract slightly, enough so that you can pull the drawer out.

What You Need
Candle or clean white bar of soap
Block plane

How to Get It Done
1. If the drawer doesn't operate smoothly when you open and close it, remove it and rub a candle or a clean white bar of soap over the top and bottom sides.
2. If that doesn't work, the drawer might have become too big for its opening. Remove the drawer and run a block plane along the top edge of the sides. Don't take off too much; remove just a bit and keep testing until the drawer operates smoothly.

Chair Fair
Tighten a Loose Chair
Time: About ½ hour

Drawers are not the only things that change in temperature and humidity can affect. The rungs and legs of chairs can also expand and contract with the seasons. That combined with the wear and tear of everyday use can loosen a chair. If not dealt with, the chair will eventually fall apart. Fixing chairs has become a way of life for me because my family and friends are always visiting for meals and games, so my big dining room table and chairs see a lot of action, all year-round. Every few months I have to round up a couple of chairs and tighten them.

What You Need
Screwdriver
Wood glue
Toothpick
Utility knife
Sandpaper
Screws
Bungee cord

How to Get It Done
1. Examine the chair to locate the loose areas. Turn the chair over and look at its joints, screws, and pegs.
2. If you spot loose screws, tighten them up and test the chair. That may solve the problem.
3. If the hole has become enlarged so that the screw no longer fits tightly in it, re-move the screw. Then put a small dab of wood glue into the hole, insert a tooth-pick into the glue, and snap or cut it off flush with the surface of the chair.
4. Now reinsert the screw and tighten it. The toothpick and glue combination gives the screw something to hold onto.

5. If a screw is missing, remove another one so you can match it for size. If the screw is missing because it fell out of a too-big hole, find or buy a screw that's just slightly bigger and longer than the one you removed. The slightly larger screw can be screwed more tightly into the expanded hole.

6. If the chair is loose because a rung has become loose or detached from its hole, you can glue and screw it back in. Gently pry apart the chair legs to loosen the rung.

7. Scrape off all traces of the old glue with a utility knife, sand the rung, and reapply wood glue to each end.

8. Apply wood glue to the holes on the chair legs.

9. Carefully put the rung back and secure it with a bungee cord to hold the legs together while the glue dries.

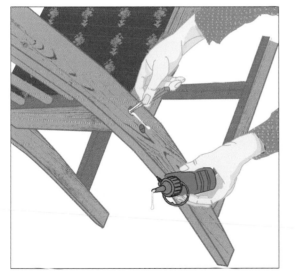

Step 3. Put a dab of glue and a toothpick into the enlarged hole.

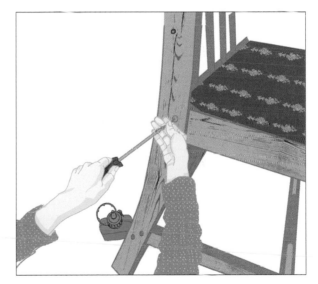

Step 4. Tighten the screw.

Getting a Leg Up
Repair a Broken Chair Leg

Time: About ½ hour for repair, about 20 minutes for repainting

Weather can impact a chair, and so can enthusiastic friends and family! I had a small group over for dinner one evening, and one of my guests leaned back in my painted wooden chair and, you guessed it, the leg broke at a jagged angle. Rather than get rid of the chair, I knew I could fix it with a little wood glue and a screw.

What You Need

Small plastic cable tie
Power drill
Tape
Paintbrushes
Wood glue
Wood screw
Rag
Wood filler
Paint or stain to match chair

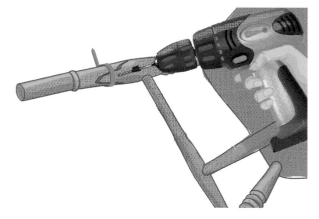

Step 3. Predrill a pilot hole.

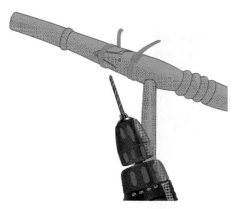

Step 4. Go back with a slightly larger drill bit and make the very top of the pilot hole slightly bigger.

How to Get It Done

1. Inspect the crack and clean it out. Get rid of any loose bits and splintering wood.
2. Line up the break and secure it temporarily with a small plastic cable tie.
3. Predrill a pilot hole for a screw that will run through the damaged area without coming out the other side. Drill from the backside of the chair at a slight angle into the damaged area. Do not go through to the other side. Mark the drill bit with a piece of tape at about half the thickness of the leg or rung that's broken.
4. Go back in with a slightly larger drill bit and make the very top of the pilot hole slightly wider so you can countersink the screw.
5. Remove the cable tie and using a paintbrush, apply wood glue to both sides of the crack. Be careful not to force the parts apart too far or the break may get larger.
6. From the backside of the chair, drive a wood screw into the repair through the pilot holes you made to bring the crack together. Drive it slightly below the surface of the wood.
7. Wipe off any glue that comes out the sides with a rag.
8. Tie another cable around the repair to hold it tightly together. You can also wrap the area with tape to hold it in place.
9. Allow the glue to set up and dry completely, overnight.
10. Cut off the cable ties or remove the tape. Fill the hole with wood filler.
11. Allow the wood filler to dry completely according to the manufacturer's instructions.
12. Repaint or stain the area. My chair was painted with a slightly distressed barn red color. The repair is virtually invisible. What seemed like a drastic break can be repaired more easily than you think.

Step 9. Let the glue dry overnight.

Improve It

Work with what you have and develop it. That's a lesson I learned very early in life. There are opportunities all around us, and we have to keep attuned to them. This goes double when it comes to enhancing your home. You can make your house your own personal palace by seeing opportunities for improvement and then going with them. The goal here is to transform what you have into something better!

Dozens of basic projects will upgrade your home with ease, and none of them require special tools, professional know-how, or even extraordinary artistic or design talent. They just necessitate seeing the possibilities in what is right in front of you. In this section I will show you a few improvements that I have found to be unique ways to beautify your home and give it great functionality. We'll start small, by changing the knobs on cabinets and furniture, and work our way up to building a mantel for a fireplace (or even for a wall where no hearth exists).

Many of these projects can be done on a quiet afternoon (I know, not exactly a common occurrence) or a rainy Sunday or anytime when you have some time to spare. Maybe you think you don't have any time to spare, but these projects are actually worth carving out part of a busy day to do. In fact, if the only way you think you can get some of them done is by scheduling them just like a meeting or a doctor's appointment, then by all means, write "change kitchen cabinet knobs" or "build shelves" in your date book or electronic calendar. That way, you will be less prone to have anything interfere with your plans. Why do I think these projects—all the projects in this book actually—are so important? Because the moments you take to complete them will give you a greater quality of life. That's worth making time for.

OPPOSITE: Here I go! Getting started on changing my boring kitchen cabinet knobs.

Before: My old, unexciting knobs

Removing the knobs only took about 30 minutes.

Get a (New) Grip
Change Your Cabinet Handles
Time: About 2 hours, depending on how many cabinets you have

You'll be surprised at how fresh your kitchen, or any cabinetry or piece of furniture for that matter, will look with this very simple-to-do update. I did it in my kitchen, and I could not believe the difference it made.

Before you go shopping, count the number of handles or knobs that need replacing. Remove one knob and screw to bring with you when you shop for replacements. Choose replacements that are secured with the same number of screws and with new screws that are the same length and diameter as the old ones. Make sure the new knobs have a larger diameter flange (the portion of the knob that rests on the surface of the wood) than the old ones. The larger knob will cover any scratches, indentations, or marks left on the face of the doors or cabinets.

If you are going from a single knob to a handle with two screws, you will have to cover up the middle hole where the original knob was with wood filler. Check out the instructions for matching stain and filling holes in "Fix a Scratch" on page 77. If your cabinets are painted, it's even easier. Simply fill the hole with joint compound, sand down, and touch up with extra paint. Because the new handle will be in front of the hole, you won't really notice the repair.

What You Need
6-in-1 interchangeable screwdriver
6-inch slip joint pliers
New cabinet pulls and screws

How to Get It Done
1. Using a screwdriver that matches the screw head (flat or Phillips), remove the old screw and knob from each door or drawer. If the screw is stripped and the screwdriver is not working to remove it, use your pliers to firmly hold the outer edge of the screw head motionless and twist the knob (counterclockwise) to remove it, taking care not to damage the cabinet.
2. Insert the new screws through the old holes and hold them tight against the back

of the door or drawer with your thumb. Twist the new knob (clockwise) onto the screw until it rests against the face of the door or drawer. Then hold the knob and tighten the screw with the screwdriver.

Screw tip: When removing and retightening screws, always remember that a clockwise turn will tighten a screw and a counterclockwise turn will loosen it (righty tighty, lefty loosey).

After: The new handles are so modern—my cabinets look brand new.

The Great Cover-Up
Paint Cabinets or Furniture
Time: Up to 2 days, depending on the number of rooms you are doing and variables in drying time

Very often, I find that older cabinets and even vintage wooden furniture are well made, but dated, dark wood finishes can sometimes give them a tired look. Even new handles or drawer pulls can't pull these pieces out of the doldrums. On the other hand, it's a shame, not to mention very costly, to replace perfectly good wooden cabinets or furniture with new versions that may not be as carefully crafted just because their finish is shot.

Paint is a wonderful way to give new life to old cabinets, even those that aren't wood. You can also paint laminate cabinetry to give it a painted wood look or simply a fresh, updated appearance. It's amazing what a new color will do! And older furniture can look surprisingly new when painted a chic color, such as a high-gloss black, a soft cream, or chocolaty satin brown. Painting furniture is a wonderful way to unify disparate pieces, too. A similar color makes different styles look right together and brings out the sculptural quality of the forms.

If you want high-shine cabinets, a true gleam can only be achieved with oil paint. Gloss finishes are modern and sophisticated-looking. The biggest plus is that gloss oil paints resist grease and dirt and are very easy to wipe down and keep clean. Satin finishes are also pretty, though not as high style, and washable. So check out samples at the home store before you buy. If you use oil or alkyd enamel paint, you must work in a well-ventilated room, and I recommend wearing a mask.

Replace the handles and knobs on newly repainted cabinets and furniture, and you really will have an entirely new room.

What You Need
Screwdriver

Plastic bag

Pencil

Warm, soapy water

Sandpaper

Power palm sander

Tack cloth

Glue

Joint compound

Wood putty

Stain-blocking primer

Mask (especially if you are using alkyd enamel paint)

Paint

Paint tray

Paint brushes in a variety of sizes

Paint thinner (to clean brushes if using oil paint)

How to Get It Done

1. If you are painting cabinets, remove all doors and keep the hinges and screws together in a plastic bag. Remove drawers. Number each door and its corresponding cabinet with a pencil.

2. Wash and dry the cabinets and furniture well with warm, soapy water. Sand down any bumps or rough spots. If the cabinets and frames have a high-gloss finish, a power palm sander will make short work of creating "tooth" on the surfaces. Primer and paint will adhere better if the cabinets are sanded smooth before proceeding. Be sure to wipe up any dust and debris with a tack cloth before painting.

3. If you are painting laminate cabinets, be sure to clean them thoroughly and remove all grease and dirt. Glue down any laminate that is lifting away from the chipboard base. If laminate is chipped, level it out with joint compound and let it dry. Sand the repair down smooth before priming.

4. Fill any other large knots, gouges, and gaps with wood putty. Sand smooth when dry.

5. Prime the cabinet or furniture with a stain-blocking primer and allow it to dry completely.

6. Paint the cabinets or furniture. Sand down and give items a second coat. Paint doors and drawers first and the face and any visible sides of the cabinets next.

7. When the doors and drawers are completely dry, about 24 hours, reinstall on cabinets.

Out on a Ledge

Painting cabinet doors or furniture isn't the only way to change the look of a room. There are a whole range of projects that can make a room go from insipid to inspiring, in no time. For example, if you have a fireplace but no mantel, or if the mantelshelf you have isn't doing anything for your decor, it's easy to change it. I found a very unusual Indonesian shelf at a salvage store. It already had brackets, so I did not have to add them. However, if you find something as basic as a beautiful piece of wood, even a piece of driftwood found on the beach, you can turn it into a unique, one-of-a-kind mantel.

Decorative brackets and corbels (a kind of ornamental bracket that projects from the wall to support a ledge or other architectural feature) can be found everywhere, from lumberyards to craft stores, so your ledge can be held up in great style. This project is so simple. Using a level will quickly and accurately assure you that you are hanging or installing any object straight. (To use a level, simply align the level on the object you are hanging and adjust it slightly until the air bubbles are centered in the indicating lines.)

Once your ledge is installed, you can really get creative. I put three beautiful framed flower photos on the ledge, taken by one of my favorite photographers. But a mantelshelf can hold all sorts of decorative and useful items: a clock, candlesticks, two or three small vases filled with fragrant flowers, family photos, and statuary . . . the possibilities are endless. When filling your mantel, keep balance and restraint in mind. You want each object to have importance, so overfilling the shelf may distract from the individual beauty of each object. The balance of texture, material, and size are three more things you want to be aware of. When you are arranging your shelf, stand back and look at it once in a while and don't be afraid to edit. And remember, of course, that you can change the arrangement whenever it strikes your fancy—once a year, once a month, or every week!

This exotic mantel gave my fireplace a whole new personality.

A Ledge-endary Lift
Install a Mantelshelf
Time: About 50 minutes

The magic of this project is all in the material you find for your shelf. Be creative with material (reclaimed wood, brand new mahogany, knotty pine) and finishes (paint, stain, distressed, waxed) to create a totally one-of-a-kind, custom look.

What You Need

Beautiful piece of wood long enough to go slightly
    beyond the width of your fireplace
Tape measure
2 to 4 decorative wood brackets, depending on
    the weight of your mantelshelf
Pencil
Expansion anchors (if applicable) (see page 6)
Safety glasses
Power drill with masonry bit and screwdriver bits
Mallet or hammer
Rag
Wood screws
Masonry screws (if applicable)
Level

How to Get It Done

1. Before you get started, determine what kind of wall you are dealing with. The wall around your fireplace will most likely be masonry unless you have a new "zero clearance" gas fireplace. In that case, the wall around it may be drywall. I do not recommend installing a mantelshelf into drywall. It should be installed into masonry or wall studs.

A mantelshelf fits together logically.

2. Measure the mantelshelf and determine how many brackets you will need. Brackets should be placed 20 to 32 inches apart. A 36-inch board is a good, basic shelf size and should require only two brackets. Anything longer or very heavy (more than 25 pounds) requires three or four brackets. Determine the overhang and mark where the braces will be placed with a pencil.

3. If you are attaching the mantelshelf to a masonry wall, use expansion anchors (see page 6) designed to hold up to 50 pounds of weight each. The weight of both the ledge and what you put on it will be carried by the strength of the anchors.

4. Put on safety glasses. Drill a hole using a masonry bit to fit the particular diameter and length of the extension anchor. When drilling into a masonry wall, I recommend operating the power drill at the highest speed and backing it out frequently to pull out masonry debris and dust that will clog the hole and overheat the drill.

5. Insert an anchor in the hole and tap it flush with the wall using a mallet or hammer covered with a rag to protect the surface of the wall. Repeat the process with the remaining anchors.

6. Place the brackets with predrilled holes to match up with the anchors you have placed in the wall. Insert standard screws of the appropriate size for the anchors into the holes and tighten.

7. If the wall is made of drywall, begin by locating the studs in the wall with a stud finder. Wall studs are 16 inches apart from each other. Decide where to mount the braces onto the wall based on the location of the studs. Use a level to align the positioning and mark the screw locations with a pencil. Secure the first bracket to the wall.

8. Place the mantel on the first bracket that has been secured to the wall. Level and align the mantel and secure the second bracket to the wall with the screws.

9. Finally, secure the brackets to the mantel.

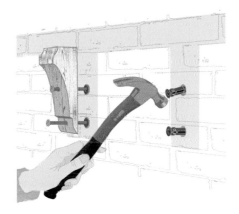

Step 5. Pound wall anchors in to hold brackets securely in masonry walls.

SAFETY NOTES

Always check with your local building department for important fire safety guidelines, especially required side and top clearance between a fireplace opening and any combustible materials. These instructions assume that if you have a fireplace, it has a noncombustible surround around the immediate firebox opening.

Fire Things Up
Build a Fireplace Mantel
Time: About 2 hours

If you love the look of your new mantelshelf and want to go a step further on your next fireplace project, consider building an entire fireplace surround. A mantel provides a decorative frame for your fireplace and a wonderful focal point. And by the way, you don't even need a real fireplace to install a mantel! Once you have it installed, simply paint the inside of the surround black, add some decorative tiles in front to simulate a hearth, add a couple of candles, and you've created a faux fireside in an otherwise plain room.

For this project, you can use a prepackaged mantel kit from a home center or lumberyard or be creative and design your own from custom-milled moldings. Have accurate measurements and make sure to have a scale sketch of your fireplace in hand when you go shopping for materials. Use your drill to make holes where the materials will be installed to determine what kind of solid backing (if any) is behind the wall where the mantel will be installed. If you are designing your own mantel, buy samples of available moldings and use wood glue to assemble short models of the sides, frieze board, and mantelshelf to help you visualize the design. When you have your design exact, ask your lumber center to mill the moldings to your specifications.

What You Need

Fireplace mantel kit or premium wood boards and custom-milled moldings
Anchors
Safety glasses
Power drill with masonry bit
Mallet or hammer
Rags
Backsaw and miter box (if applicable)
Wood glue
Nails
Sandpaper
Painter's tape
Stain and polyurethane or primer and trim paint
Steel wool

How to Get It Done

1. Attach the wood surround to the wall using appropriate fasteners. If you are attaching the surround to a masonry wall, use expansion anchors. Locate the fasteners where they will be covered by moldings.

2. Put on safety glasses. Drill a hole using a masonry bit to fit the particular diameter and length of the extension anchor. When drilling into a masonry wall, I recommend operating the power drill at the highest speed and backing it out frequently to pull out masonry debris and dust that will clog the hole and overheat the drill.

3. Insert the anchor in the hole and tap it flush with the wall using a mallet or hammer covered with a rag to protect the surface of the wall. Repeat the process with the remaining anchors.

4. Because you followed the golden rule of "measure twice, cut once" when ordering your custom-cut moldings, everything will fit precisely. If not, you may need a backsaw and miter box to make adjustments. Glue all joints, wiping off any excess glue with a damp cloth. Glue on the wood will prevent the stain from adhering properly. Attach the molding to the surround with finishing nails. Countersink any visible nails.

5. Sand and clean the surface of the mantel. Tape off the wall and adjoining areas with painter's tape. Apply stain, then smooth the surface with steel wool before applying at least three coats of polyurethane or other protective coating. If painting, use a primer, followed by two or more coats of trim paint. Make sure all the products you are using are heat-resistant.

Step 1. Attach the wood surround to the wall.

Clutter Command

Clutter equals stress, plain and simple.

Messy rooms, disorganized closets, and jumbled junk drawers add unneeded hassle to our already hectic days. I can't think when things are cluttered! So I've learned a few tricks to control the clutter. I sort and toss the stuff I don't need or want, and I keep the necessities of life tucked away, out of site but easily accessible.

Even small homes have space for storage. Under the bed, at the back of a closet, under the sink—all these spaces can be used to hold out-of-season clothes, toys, sports equipment, and unsightly trash bins. That's right, even putting the kitchen trash bin under the sink and on a convenient roll-out trolley, instead of having it out in plain sight, reduces both visual and floor space clutter.

Donating useful but no longer needed items, getting rid of unwanted junk, and keeping what we do need neat, accessible, and as invisible as possible let our personal spaces become welcoming havens instead of uninviting areas that make you want to run away. In an ideal world, every room of your house should be neat as a pin and organized alphabetically. But we know that's pretty much impossible. After all, we do have to live our lives, and making a mess is sometimes part of it. But the storage solutions in this section can help you keep your stuff restrained.

Simple shelves, for instance, are one of the most basic and useful forms of storage. Tucked into the back of a closet, at the end of a little used hallway, or in the corner of a child's bedroom, they provide an easy, classic clutter solution. They can hold decorative bins, boxes, and baskets for all the stuff you need but don't want to look at. Or hang a curtain in front of them for complete coverage but easy access. Once you see how easy shelves are to install, you'll find all sorts of places for them.

Basic shelves are easy and inexpensive to construct using wood, plywood, or fiberboard cut to specific lengths and widths and hanging them from metal shelving standards (long metal strips that hold brackets) and arm brackets. For a less utilitarian look, you can attach shelves to decorative brackets. Consider saving time and skipping the cutting and sanding steps by taking your measurements to the lumberyard or home improvement store and having them cut the wood to your specifications. It costs a little extra for the cuts, but it may be worth it if you are short on time and tools.

Basic shelves can be made from a variety of materials. If the shelves are going in a closet or utility area (such as a laundry or mudroom), ¼-inch plywood or pine shelves can be sanded smooth and then left as is. Plywood sheets are less costly than solid wood boards. Keep in mind that plywood does not normally come in shelf-width planks, but in 4- by 8-foot sheets, which need to be cut or "ripped" into shelf width. Unless you have a circular saw and know how to use it, you will have to have plywood sheets cut into shelves at the home center or lumberyard when you purchase the sheets. For a finished look, you can add veneer tape to the front and sides of plywood shelves. It's easy to apply with an iron because it is coated with a heat-activated adhesive.

If you are planning on making the shelves a prominent feature of a room, you can paint or stain them to match your color and design scheme. For a high-end look, sheets of plywood veneer (plywood covered with birch, mahogany, cherry, or even oak sheathing) can be cut to size and coated with polyurethane for a natural finished look, stained, or even painted. And, of course, you can buy hardwood boards, such as aspen, oak, or cherry, but these woods are expensive. Plywood veneer gives you the same look for a lot less. You can also buy melamine-coated particleboard shelving (usually available already cut in a variety of standard widths and lengths) if you want an easy-to-clean surface.

Shelve It!
Build Simple Shelves Hung on Metal Shelving Standards
Time: About 2 hours, depending on how many shelves you hang

I installed adjustable shelves in a closet behind my kitchen, essentially turning it into a pantry. I store lots of soft drinks, juice, cereal, and other dry goods on those shelves. And I keep Zach's favorite healthy snacks and juices on lower shelves, so they are easy for him to grab. The pantry closet also gives me more space in my kitchen cabinets.

What You Need

Stud finder

Pencil

Tape measure

Plywood, wood, or melamine-coated shelves cut to length in 1- by 8-inch, 1- by 10-inch, or 1- by 12-inch wide boards, according to size and quantity needs

Crosscut saw (or a circular saw if you have one and know how to use it)

Sandpaper or power palm sander

Metal shelving standards (appropriate screws are included) cut to height of all shelves*

Metal arm brackets (twice the number of shelves you are planning on hanging)

Strips of 1- by 2-inch clear pine or hardwood cut to the same length as the metal shelving standards

Polyurethane (optional)

Paint or stain (optional)

Spray paint (optional)

Paint brush (optional)

Power screwdriver with drill bit attachments

3-inch wallboard screws

Carpenter's level

* Metal shelving standards and arm brackets come in a small array of colors, including plain silver tone metal, white, black, and brown. If you are planning on painting or staining shelves, choose a color that blends in best or spray paint the standards to match the color you are painting the shelves.

Step 1. Use a stud finder to locate wall studs.

How to Get It Done

1. Locate the wall studs where you want your shelves with a stud finder and mark the spots with a pencil. To be truly secure, shelves are best installed into wall studs. For heavy loads, attach a standard to every stud along the span of the shelf. If you have to attach the shelves between studs, use appropriate anchors and do not exceed the manufacturer's recommended load limits for between-stud installation.

2. Using a tape measure, determine the width and length of the shelves you need. The length of the shelves should overhang the brackets by 4 inches.

3. Cut or have shelves cut to the chosen length (and in the case of plywood, width).

4. Cut or have cut two or three strips of 1- by 2-inch clear pine or hardwood to the same length as the metal shelving standards. For shelves that will span more than 36 inches, use three strips and standards.

5. If you are planning on painting, staining, or coating the shelves with polyurethane, do that now to both the shelves and the strips (and the metal standards and arms, if you like). Let them dry completely before proceeding.

6. Position the metal standards in the middle of the 1- by 2-inch strips and attach them using the screws provided with or recommended by the manufacturer.

7. Attach the strips with standards to the wall studs with 3-inch wallboard screws. Make sure that the openings in the standards that hold the arm brackets (that hold the shelves) match up on either side of the strips, otherwise the shelves will not hang level. Use a carpenter's level to make sure that the standards are plumb so the arm brackets will be level.

8. Attach the arm brackets and place the shelves on top. The beauty of using metal shelving standards and brackets is they allow you to add more shelves as you need them, and you can also adjust their height.

Step 8. Adjustable brackets allow you to place shelves where *you* want them.

Build Simple Shelves Hung on Decorative Brackets
Time: About 2 hours, depending on how many shelves you hang

Pretty brackets turn basic shelves into something good-looking enough to show off in a living room or dining room.

What You Need
Stud finder

Pencil

Tape measure

Plywood, wood, or melamine-coated shelves cut to length in 1- by 8-inch, 1- by 10-inch, or 1- by 12-inch wide boards, according to size and quantity needs

Crosscut saw (or a circular saw if you have one and know how to use it)

Polyurethane (optional)

Paint or stain (optional)

Spray paint (optional)

Paint brush (optional)

Sandpaper or power palm sander

Metal, wrought iron, or wooded brackets

Power screwdriver with drill bit attachments

3-inch wallboard screws

Carpenter's level

How to Get It Done
1. Using a stud finder, locate the wall studs where you want your shelves and mark the spots with a pencil. To be truly secure, shelves are best installed into wall studs. For heavy loads, attach a standard to every stud along the span of the shelf. If you have to attach the shelves between studs, use appropriate anchors and do not exceed the manufacturer's recommended load limits for between-stud installation.
2. Using a tape measure, determine the width and length of the shelves you need. The length of the shelves should overhang the brackets by 4 inches.

3. Cut or have shelves cut to your chosen length (and in the case of plywood, width).

4. If you are planning on painting, staining, or coating the shelves with polyurethane, do that now to both the shelves and the brackets. Let them dry completely before proceeding.

5. Attach one shelf bracket for every 16 inches of shelf span, depending on the weight of items you plan on putting on the shelves (i.e., framed photos don't carry as much weight as books do).

6. Level the shelf brackets using a carpenter's level. If necessary, hold the level on a 2×4 to level wide spans.

7. Lay the shelves on top of the brackets.

Shelves can hold all sorts of things and still look great.

Pot Luck
Hang a Ceiling Pot Rack
Time: About 40 minutes

Storing my pots and pans in my undercounter cabinets and drawers was not only inconvenient, but inevitably, my favorite sauté pan would end up in the far reaches of the bottom drawer, making it difficult to reach. Plus, the bulky pots took up a lot of valuable space. My solution? Hanging a pot rack from the ceiling. Not only did it free up more space, I can now see what I need and grab it easily. The most important aspect of hanging a pot rack in the ceiling is making sure the large molly bolts that go into the ceiling and hold the rack (that holds the pans) go into ceiling beams or joists. Most kits are sized to expand the width of ceiling joists, which is every 16 inches.

The rack you choose will come with instructions. There are different kinds of pot racks and each kind has specific installation methods. Please follow the manufacturer's instructions. Here's what you can expect if you install a hanging pot rack like mine.

My new pot rack gives my kitchen a professional look.

What You Need
Ladder
Safety glasses
Stud finder
Cardboard (you can use the box the rack came in)
Hanging ceiling pot rack kit
Pencil
Painter's tape
Power drill with screwdriver bits
Wrench or pliers with rubber-coated handle

How to Get It Done
1. Because you'll be standing on a ladder, make sure the area you are working on is clear! When working with anything above your head, make sure the work is 12 to 16 inches in front of you.

Opposite: New cabinet pulls, a hanging pot rack . . . all straightforward projects that made my kitchen feel new and fresh—and ready for entertaining!

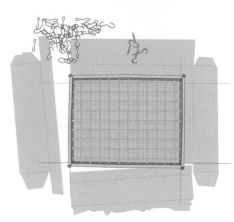

Step 3. Make a template for the pot rack using the cardboard box the kit came in.

2. Wear safety glasses.

3. Locate the ceiling joists, using a stud finder. Then, using the cardboard from the hanging ceiling pot rack kit, make a template using the outside of the rack as a guide. Make holes (use a pencil to poke through the cardboard) where the four ceiling hooks that come with the kit are located for attaching the rack to the ceiling.

4. Tape the template to the ceiling with painter's tape, making sure that the holes you made are placed in the middle of the width of the ceiling joist location.

5. Use a pencil to mark the four corner holes on the ceiling. This will be where you will drill.

6. Drill holes using the bit size the manufacturer recommends and then screw in the heavy eyehooks that will hold the chain of the rack. For leverage, use a rubber-coated handle of a wrench to turn the hooks. It won't mar the chrome or finish of the hook and it will save your hands!

7. Next, hang the chains that attach to the rack. It's best if the rack is placed at a height that's easy for the cook in the house to reach. Be mindful of how far your pans with long handles will hang. You may have to try a couple of chain lengths before you get it right.

8. Once everything is in place, hang your pots!

Step 7. Hang the rack.

On a Roll
Install a Trash Bin Trolley
Time: Less than 30 minutes

Another way to clean up your kitchen and give yourself more floor space at the same time is by installing a trash trolley or pull out waste bin underneath your sink. Who wants to stare at a trash bin when they're eating anyway? Not me! Installing a trash bin trolley, available at most home stores, makes the bin even easier and cleaner to access. If the bin glides out easily, children and others will be less likely to open the cabinet door and toss the trash in and miss the basket in the process. And the easy gliding action of the trolley lets you pull it out when you're cooking and toss waste into the basket easily.

The kits are easy to install with just a screwdriver! One caveat: Measure the space before you buy to make sure that the trolley will not interfere with any pipes or hoses under the sink. Most kits come with the appropriate-size wastebasket. It may be smaller than the one you are using now. I think having a smaller wastebasket in the kitchen in a good idea. You're less likely to have a lot of trash in the kitchen if the bag gets filled up faster. Take it out to the curb, where it belongs!

What You Need
Pull-out trash bin kit
Pencil
Power drill with screwdriver bits

How to Get It Done
1. Remove the bin from the trolley.
2. Place the trolley in the location under the sink.
3. Using a pencil, mark the screw holes and remove the trolley.
4. Drill pilot holes on the four marks.
5. Place the trolley assembly back, lining up the pilot holes with the holes in the trolley.
6. Screw the trolley in place. Make sure it glides easily in and out.
7. Place the bin inside, line with a trash bin liner, and start using it!

A trash trolley keeps kitchen waste out of the way.

Closet Control

My trash trolley and new pot rack completed my "renovated" kitchen. They, along with closet pantry shelves, new knobs, and drawer pulls, were really all it needed to look neat and up-to-date. Once I saw the dramatic results in my kitchen, I wanted to make changes elsewhere. The bedroom was a logical choice for me because I have lots of clothes, shoes, and accessories that need to be accessible but stored neatly away.

My closet was a logical place to start. I had old wire shelves and poles, and they just were not working for me. I have a walk-in closet in my bedroom, but it's not especially deluxe or large. Many of you probably have similar closets. After I found out how much it costs to have a professional closet company come in and redo just one closet in my house, I knew I had to come up with a better, less expensive way. Luckily, most home centers, large discount retailers, and specialty organizing stores now sell all the do-it-yourself components you need to create storage-friendly closets.

Once my new closet was in place and filled with the season's clothing, I still had to find a place to stow out-of-season outfits. I have a guest room with a traditional bed with loads of room underneath it. While cardboard under-the-bed storage boxes are inexpensive, they are not especially sturdy or attractive. I knew I could turn some old dresser drawers into long-lasting, customized storage units on wheels. You can use the drawers from a bureau you're getting rid of, or find them at a local thrift store. Before you start, measure the space under your bed to make sure the drawer slides easily under it—and factor in the height of the wheels. (The casters may add up to 2 inches.) New handles and a coat of paint (inside and out because the drawers will be pulled out some of the time) will also make them look less like a drawer and more like a customized storage box.

Closet Case
Organize a Closet
Time: Less than 1 day (not including shopping time!)

Redoing a closet doubles its space capabilities.

What You Need
- Screwdriver
- Joint compound or spackle
- Sandpaper
- Paint
- Paintbrush
- Tape measure
- Flat pack closet organizer shelves and pole units

How to Get It Done

1. Remove any old shelving and poles from the closet. Use a screwdriver, if necessary, to remove units that are screwed to the wall.
2. Patch any holes in the drywall that your "demolition" left behind with joint compound or spackle and sand with sandpaper. (See "Patch Small to Medium Holes in Drywall" on page 49 for wall-patching how-to.)
3. Apply a fresh coat of paint and allow it to dry before proceeding.
4. Measure the dimensions of the closet height, width, and depth and take them to a home center or retailer that sells closet systems. Choose a combination of shelving and poles that fit your needs and your closet.
5. Most units will come "flat packed" and are assembled with an Allen wrench, which is usually included with the kit.
6. Assemble the kit according to the manufacturer's instructions and install it in your closet.

Before: My old closet wasted a lot of valuable storage space.

After: Assembly of my new closet system was easy, and you can see what a huge difference it made—at a fraction of the cost of a custom job.

Under-Cover Operation
Create an Under-the-Bed Storage Box
Time: Less than 1 hour, plus drying time

The space under your bed is one big empty parking lot. Fill it up with *these* storage "wheels."

What You Need

Old drawer

Soapy water for cleaning

Clean rags or paper towels

Fine sandpaper

Screwdriver or power drill with screwdriver bits

New handle (optional)

Wood putty (if necessary when changing handle)

Stain-blocking primer

Paintbrushes

Latex paint (your choice of color)

Four plastic screw-on casters

Pencil

Enough canvas or denim to cover the length and width of the drawer (any sturdy fabric that coordinates with the color of your drawer)

Tape measure

Scissors

Sewing machine or fabric glue (available at any craft store)

Velcro strips

How to Get It Done

1. Clean your drawer inside and out with mild soapy water. Dry it with clean rags or paper towels, then sand down any rough spots with fine sandpaper. Wipe away any sawdust with a barely damp paper towel.

2. Remove the handle from the drawer with a screwdriver. If you're using the existing handle, set it and the screws aside in a safe place. If you're using a new handle that doesn't match the existing holes, fill those holes with wood putty,

BARBARA'S BEST-KEPT SECRET

If you're storing woolens or other natural fabrics, cedar balls or bars, available at most department and home stores, are a kid-friendly, environmentally safe way to discourage moths from chowing down on your favorite clothes.

BOXING DAY

Under-the-bed storage boxes aren't just for sweaters and other out-of-season stuff. Here are some other items you may want to keep tucked away:

- Home office equipment if you have a small space and don't want to look at your work all the time
- Shoes, shoes, and more shoes
- Small- and medium-size sports equipment, such as hand weights, jump rope, or yoga mat
- Serving platters and other serving and entertaining items you don't use all that often but need access to when you *do* entertain!
- Tools and home repair items
- Light bulbs, extension cords, and other pesky (but necessary) household items
- Photographs and memorabilia

let the putty dry, and sand it down. If your new handles *do* match the existing holes, don't paint over the openings.

3. Paint the drawer inside and out—except for the bottom—with a stain-blocking primer. It will cover up knotholes, stain, or finish on the drawer front and give you a clean base to start. After the primer is dry (about 1 hour), paint the drawer with your favorite color or design. Let the paint dry completely before proceeding, about 2 hours.

4. Mark the caster placement: one caster in each corner. The wood on the bottom of your drawer should be soft enough to screw into easily. If it's not, mark the screw holes with a pencil. Put pressure on the marks with your screwdriver to make small indentations, called pilot holes, to make it easier to drive the screw in with your screwdriver.

5. Attach your casters to all four corners with a screwdriver or power drill with screwdriver bits, using the pilot holes as a guide.

6. Reattach the drawer handle. If you're using new handles, mark the screw holes, drill, and attach the new handle with a screwdriver.

Step 1. Sand down any rough spots in the drawer to get a smooth surface for painting.

Step 3. Prime and paint the drawer.

7. For long-term storage, protect your things with a cover. Choose a sturdy fabric, such as heavyweight canvas. You can also use denim or another heavy-duty fabric.

8. Measure the top of the drawer front to back and side to side, using the top of the sides and the back as a starting point. The goal is for the fabric to sit on top of the sides and back and just meet the front of the drawer. The drawer front is usually higher than the sides and back, and because you want the fabric to sit flat, you will attach the fabric only to the sides and back.

9. Cut a piece of fabric 1 inch larger than the measurement all the way around.

10. Hem the fabric by turning it under ½ inch twice all the way around so the hemmed fabric sits on top of the sides and back rail of the drawer and just meets the front of the drawer. Sew or tack down the hem with fabric glue.

11. Attach self-stick Velcro strips right on top of the two sides and back edge of the drawer. The width of the Velcro might be slightly wider than the drawer sides. If this is the case, simply press the Velcro so it fits snuggly on the sides. Take the Velcro tape off the top piece, lay the fabric on top, and attach.

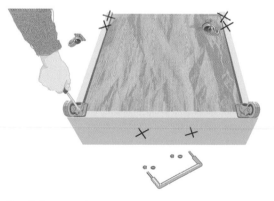

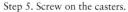
Step 5. Screw on the casters.

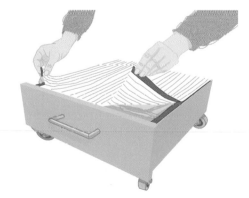

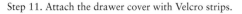
Step 11. Attach the drawer cover with Velcro strips.

Entryway Welcome

Organizing rooms and closets using some of the suggestions here will bring a new sense of order to day-to-day living. It is remarkable that simply having things in order and in a place where they can be easily located can be so good for your soul. There is one area of the house that I haven't talked about, and it's one that I think is often neglected: the entryway.

There's nothing worse than stepping into your house and being greeted with trash bins, toys, assorted jackets and shoes, the litter box, rubber dog toys, and so on? Come on. You know *exactly* what I mean!

The front entrance is so important: It's the first impression you and your guests have of your home. The entryway should make the transition from the outside world to your private space a smooth and welcoming one. Keeping it neat, pretty, personal, and functional is key. That way, the minute you come through the door, you can relax and the cares of the day can be left on the doorstep.

Before: My old entryway wasn't very hospitable.

Opposite: *After:* A place to sit, a mirror to do a last minute lipstick check before a big date, some lovely lighting, and favorite books and keepsakes give my entryway a lot of "Wow!"

A pillow for the stool changes the look of the entryway table.

Enter Organized
Organize an Entryway
Time: ½ day (or 1 day if you paint the hallway)

Here are the elements of a happy, warm, and welcoming foyer, and they can be used in even the smallest of entries.

What You Need
Bench or small chair

Side table

Lamp

Plant(s)

Small clock

Personal items, such as special photos or mementos

How to Get It Done
1. Clear everything out of your entryway. Use another room as a "staging area" to sort through what you have.
2. Clean the entryway and repaint, if necessary.
3. Start going through the items that were in your entryway. Store anything that doesn't belong in the entryway (tools, toys, etc.) in an appropriate place. (How about on those shelves you built or in the under-the-bed storage boxes you made?)
4. Start adding back essential items. Consider a bench or small chair. It's both useful and beautiful. A couple of pillows make it the perfect place to put on or take off shoes. A side table is perfect for setting down a package. It can be a long sideboard or a tall, round candle stand. Be sure to add a small bowl for keys and a basket for mail. A lamp adds an extra source of light, brightens up a dark hall, and highlights personal items displayed on the table. Plants add life—literally—to a space. Be sure to select a plant that does well in low light, such as a philodendron. A clock will be helpful so you know if you're running late! Finally, add personal touches such as a favorite picture, some sea shells that remind you of a special beach vacation, or small collections to act as happy reminders for you and serve as focal points of your life for visitors.

IT'S TIME TO VENT!

You may have large wall vents that blow hot and cold air into your house as part of its heating and cooling system. Great system, unattractive vents! So how can you minimize the visual impact of these utilitarian features? Cover them up, or course. Now, you cannot completely cover vents with a solid material. That will defeat their purpose (and keep you pretty cold in the winter). But you can disguise them very easily.

First, paint the vent the same color as your wall. Most vents are metal so they need to be sanded lightly and then primed before the final coat goes on. Once you have that done, stand back and see if it's not enough of a cover-up to make you happy. If not, try my trick with beaded or shell curtains. I found mine at a home design store (see Resources on page 250 for details)—but large retailers also carry them.

Because my wall vents are quite large, I bought extra shell curtains and cut up one set and tied each strand to the bottom on the ones I hung. That way they reached the floor and created a long, elegant seamless look. In order to keep the shells from blowing around and sounding like a wind chime (the biggest in the world!), I took a clear plastic dowel and tied the bottom of the strands to it. I secured the dowel to the floor with double-stick tape. It's really that easy!

The vents are less noticeable now.

The delicate shells add a fascinating element of texture and light movement to the entryway.

Get Comfortable in a Clutter-Free Zone!

Finally, after everything is put away and you feel completely decluttered, take a moment and think about yourself. Everyone needs a comfortable, beautiful spot to call her own. Carve out a niche wherever you can find it—in a spare bedroom, a corner of your family room, or even a back porch or sunroom. It's so important to have a place to retreat to when things get hectic. For me, it's just a corner of my living room, blocked off by simple sheers and a wooden panel hung from the ceiling to create another "room" within a room.

I found an exotic daybed, and that really is all there is to my little sanctuary. I wrapped a standard twin-size mattress in a pretty length of silk and topped it with lots of soft pillows in luxurious fabrics. (Pillows are a great way to decorate; they're affordable and easy to change by whim or season.) Colorful lanterns hung from the ceiling and two plump leather ottomans give the area an exotic feel. A sturdy coffee table to hold books and a cool drink make the space practical, too. Anyone can do this, even on a smaller scale. A comfortable chair and footrest, some pillows and a comfortable throw, and a pretty reading lamp can turn any corner into a clutter-free retreat.

If a little guilt is creeping in about making a space for yourself, remember that giving yourself the gift of quiet and order is one that reverberates and reaches everyone in your life. If you take a moment for yourself to reflect in comfortable, tidy surroundings, you will be so much more ready to face the challenges of the day. Every morning, whenever I can, I sip some tea and focus my mind while sitting cross-legged in my daybed. It's a wonderful way to start my day.

OPPOSITE: This simple screen, found at a flea market, creates just enough privacy for my special living room sanctuary.

Panel Magic
Create a Private Space
Time: About 30 minutes per panel

Add a personal flare by using beads or vintage jewelry as tiebacks for your fabric panel.

Creating a private nook for my daybed was easy, and it didn't require the construction of any additional walls. I hung an antique wood panel I found at a flea market from the ceiling and flanked it with fabric panels that are sewn onto wooden rods. The clear filament makes the panel appear as if it's just floating in the room.

It's also possible to sew a pocket at the top of your fabric panel and run it on a curtain rod. Filament can be tied to each end of the rod and attached to the ceiling with cup hooks, if the rod is not too heavy Or you can attach curtain rods right to the ceiling.

I pulled back one of the fabric panels like a curtain with a simple cup hook screwed into the wall and a beaded tieback. You can make one yourself by stringing beads or even by using a vintage beaded necklace. It's totally unique jewelry for your room! Hanging the panels is deceptively easy, too.

What You Need
- Fabric or wood panels
- Rods or bars to hang fabric from
- 1½-inch wood screws
- Cup hooks
- Heavy-duty clear filament or fishing line
- Power screwdriver
- Joint compound
- Putty knife
- Fine sandpaper
- Ladder
- Beads or old vintage beaded necklace
- Fishing wire to strong beads
- Cup hooks (to hold the tie back in place)

How to Get It Done

1. Locate the running length of the ceiling joist.
2. Choose where along the length of the joist you want to hang your panel.
3. I screwed cup hooks into the top of my wooden panel. Then I measured the distance between the two hooks and transferred those measurements to the ceiling.
4. Once you have made the corresponding marks in the ceiling, wrap heavy-duty clear filament around a 1½-inch wood screw. Make sure there's plenty of length to the filament. I actually used fishing line right off Zachary's fishing pole! You can always cut it to size later. Better to have a good length to work with.
5. Next, make pilot holes in the ceiling then install the screws with the filament attached, into the pilot holes. Drive the screws in just below the surface and let the filament hang down.
6. Fill in the indentations created by the screws with joint compound. (See "Patch Small to Medium Holes in Drywall" on page 49 for instructions on filling holes.)
7. Next, tie the filament to the cup hooks on the panel to the desired height. Voila! Instant privacy.

You've done it—your place is looking great! Everything is running smoothly, it's freshly painted and organized, and the décor expresses your personality. Let's not stop here—let's take it outside!

SAFETY NOTE:

Take care when working on a ladder. Make sure the area you are working on is clear! When working with anything above your head, make sure the work is 12 to 16 inches in front of you.

Chapter 8
The Great Outdoors

Zachary is a very active 7-year-old, so having a backyard that's safe and fun to use is important to me. Those of you with children know that they love to feel free to run, throw balls, and play with their friends. Childhood is so short, and the world is so complicated. I want Zach to enjoy being a kid, especially in the summer, when school's out and summer vacation seems to stretch before him like an endless journey of catching frogs, spitting watermelon seeds, and swimming in the ocean. *These* are the experiences that children remember forever—not the day they received the latest toy or computer game.

You don't have to have a prize-winning vegetable patch or grow temperamental perennials to have a nice yard that children and adults can enjoy. Elaborate gardens and demanding planting beds aren't for me. Just keep it basic, clean, and green! I adore flowers, especially tall ones that blow in the wind, but even they can be kept low-maintenance in window boxes and attractive pots around the door and patio. I want to enjoy my outside time with Zachary, so finding a way to make my back-yard practical, easy to care for, pretty, and fun for both of us (as well as our friends and family) is important to me.

I take a simple approach, one that I think works for everyone (especially for those of you who may not have the greenest thumbs). I have a fairly large expanse of lawn. My planting beds are modest and stocked with low-maintenance evergreens and flowering shrubs. I laid a flagstone walk on the side of my house leading to a back door. It's a pleasant and secure way for everyone to come and go, and it also adds interesting but simple landscaping detail to the property. Because we live close to the ocean, I had an outside shower installed by a licensed plumber and then built a privacy surround for it. The outdoor shower keeps sandy feet from tracking inside.

Maintaining the exterior of your house and outdoor tools is part of keeping your house neat and lending it some curb appeal. It's pretty easy to keep up with the great outdoors, beautify it without breaking the bank, and still have time to bask in the sun!

SAFETY NOTES

Remember to always follow manufacturer's instructions when using any product or tool, even if you've used it in the past. Manufacturers take a lot of time to write user-friendly instructions, and they know better than anyone about how to use their particular material or tool. Also use safety glasses when working with hammers and mallets. And when lifting anything heavy, use your knees, not your back, to do the work! Oh, and don't forget the sunscreen! There's nothing fun about a painful and potentially damaging sunburn.

A Fresh Look at Maintenance

I don't have hours and hours to devote to keeping up with my yard. I'd rather take Zach to the beach, enjoy leisurely outdoor meals with my family or a boyfriend, or just relax on a lounge chair and read a magazine. I inspect and maintain the house and walkways, mow the lawn (or pay a local teenager to do it), and water the flowers in a couple of hours on Saturday mornings. That's really all it takes to keep the yard looking good. I leave major annual projects, such as painting the house trim and cleaning and maintaining my home's wood shingle siding, to the pros. Fall cleanup and winter prep takes a bit more time. But it's only once a year, and if you're feeling pressed, you can hire someone to help you out in those areas.

OPPOSITE: Your yard is one big blank canvas—you can transform it without spending a fortune on landscape designers or expensive plants.

Love Your Tools!

It doesn't matter how great your yard looks: If your garden tools aren't in good shape, it's not going to stay that way. The best way to make sure your tools last a long time is to clean them after use and then store them correctly. The elements—rain and snow, changing temperatures, and humidity—can wreak havoc on tools. Metal parts can rust, and wooden handles can split and break.

Gather the following items to have on hand when you need to repair or maintain garden tools.

Rags	Garden tote
Linseed or mineral oil	Pail
Rubbing alcohol	Sand
Soap and water	Metal or plastic trash bin
Spray-on lubricant	Hose
Fine sandpaper	Wall-mounted hose reel
Hockey tape	Chalk

- Trowels, cultivators, hand weeders, rakes, and shovels should be immediately cleaned of dirt, leaves, and other debris after use. After that, apply a light coat of linseed or mineral oil to all the metal parts of the tools, including the handle joints. Be sure to wipe the blades of cutters with rubbing alcohol after each use to avoid spreading disease from plant to plant. Clean pruning shears with a soap-and-water scrub and dry thoroughly, paying special attention to the joints and gears. Use a spray-on lubricant on the gears to prevent rust and ensure smooth cutting the next time you use them.
- If the wooden handles of your tools have lost their finish or have dried out, go over them lightly with fine sandpaper and then rub linseed or mineral oil into them with a clean rag. If the handle is cracked or split, but the joints are sturdy and the blades or tines are still in good shape, don't

throw the tool out. Instead, starting at the joint where the blade or tines meet the handle, wrap the handle with hockey tape. It's very sturdy and has give, which allows for a very tight wrap. You can buy hockey tape at sporting goods stores.

- For short-term storage during the growing season, keep small tools handy in a garden tote in a protected, dry area. For long term storage, place metal hand tools blades-down in a pail of sand mixed with a small amount of linseed or mineral oil (about 2 gallons of sand to 1 cup of oil).
- Store large tools such as rakes and shovels handle side down in a clean metal or plastic trash bin. You can also buy wall brackets specially made for hanging tools on a pegboard rack. (See "Make a Peg-Board Storage Rack" on page 4.)
- After you've finished mowing the lawn, hose off clippings that are stuck on top of the mower. Keep mower blades lubricated to make sure they operate well and resist rust. Don't store mowers outside. If you don't have a garage or shed, keep them covered and in a protected area. Water is the lawn mower's worst enemy. Riding mowers require an oil change at least once a season and as often as after every five uses; gas-powered push mowers need to have their oil changed every season, at least. Riding mowers should also have a year-end tune-up, which will forestall a disaster the following year.
- Store your hose on a wall-mounted reel to keep it tidy and off the ground after and between watering. Kinking and laying on rough surfaces cause most hose problems. When you pause for more than a few minutes in watering, turn the hose off at the faucet. Relying on the spray nozzle's shut-off valve allows water pressure to build up, and that in turn can cause leaks. In the winter, drain the hose, then remove it from the spout and store it in a basement, utility room, or garage. If the hose is left outside, freezing and thawing may also cause the hose to crack and leak.

Hose Sweet Hose
Fix a Leaky Hose
Time: 10 to 15 minutes

If your hose springs a leak, there's no need to replace it. First, identify the location of the leak: Place the hose on a flat surface, such as a driveway, and turn it on. Mark the leaking area with a piece of chalk. Turn the hose off and dry it so you can make the repair.

What You Need
Waterproof duct tape
Utility knife
Plastic couplings and connectors
Liquid dish soap

How to Get It Done
1. Pinholes and small cracks can be wrapped with waterproof duct tape. Wrap the damaged area plus at least 1 inch past the damage in both directions, making tight overlapping spirals. Do not pull the tape so tightly that it flattens the hose or stretches too much. If it's a very hot day, more than 80°F, make the repair in a cool place, such as a garage, or at least in the shade. The heat may make the hose expand and distort the repair.
2. For larger breaks, you will have to cut the hose and create a watertight connection with couplings. Use a sharp utility knife to cut the damaged section from the hose. Make the cut as straight as possible. Ragged cuts may inhibit a good connection. Take the damaged piece to a home center and use it to find the right size replacement couplings. Make sure the couplings fit the diameter and material of your hose. Some hoses are made of rubber and others of vinyl. Couplings are sometimes made for one material or the other.
3. Attach the male and female couplings to the cut ends, following the manufacturer's instructions.
4. If the fittings don't slide in easily, soften the hose in hot water and lubricate it with some liquid dish soap.

PREPARE FOR WINTER

- Clean terra-cotta and clay pots with a mixture of 1 part bleach to 9 parts water inside and out with a sturdy sponge. Turn them over.
- Clear leaves and debris from around home's foundation to discourage rodents from burrowing there.
- Turn off the outside water supply but keep the faucet open to allow remaining water to drain off and prevent freeze damage.
- Clear the gutters of leaves and other debris.
- Bag fallen leaves and discard them or add them to a compost heap (if you're so inclined). Many towns pick up bagged leaves and make their own community compost. Check with your local sanitation or extension service for details.
- Store away or cover lawn furniture and grill.
- Cover air-conditioning units.
- Put up storm windows.
- Mulch large shrubs after the first hard frost. (Doing it earlier will encourage rodents to burrow in the warm blanket of wood chips.)
- Inspect concrete patios, driveways, and foundations and patch any cracks.

Hard Facts about Cracks
Patch a Hairline Crack in Concrete
Time: 20 minutes to 1 hour, depending on the size of the crack, plus drying time

Maintaining the exterior of your house and its grounds includes taking care of patios, driveways, and the exposed area of your home's foundation. Inevitably, cracks will occur in these areas, and they should be filled and repaired before they become too big to fix.

For fine concrete cracks, you can try using a new product on the market, which is specifically made for filling in small cracks. It is a cement product that is sold under various brand names, but generically it's called—simply enough—premixed concrete patch. It comes in tubs and tubes and needs no special preparation. Basically, you squeeze it into a clean opening and let it cure according to the package directions. You can also repair hairline cracks with a grout made of portland cement and water. (Portland cement is a type of cement made by heating and then pulverizing limestone and clay to a sandy consistency. Its basic ingredient is concrete.) Add enough water to the cement to form a thick paste and follow my directions.

What You Need
Garden hose with spray nozzle
Premixed concrete patch (usually sold in a tube or a tub)
   or portland cement and water mixture
Putty knife or trowel
Plastic drop cloth
Scrap piece of 1×4 lumber

How to Get It Done
1. Clean the crack out by using the most powerful setting on your hose's spray nozzle. This will also moisten the concrete, which will prevent it from drawing the water from the grout and drying out the mixture. Although the old concrete should be moist, no water should be standing on the surface or in the crack when the concrete patch is applied.
2. Apply the concrete patch or mixture of portland cement and water with a putty knife or trowel. Force the patch into the crack as much as possible.
3. Then, using the scrap lumber, smooth it so it is level with the original concrete.

Step 2. Apply the concrete mix to the crack.

Step 3. Smooth out the concrete with a scrap of lumber.

4. Allow the patched area to dry for about 2 hours. Then cover the area with a piece of plastic drop cloth.
5. Keep the area covered for about 5 days. Lift the covering once each day and sprinkle the area with water.

Patch a Large Crack in Concrete

Time: 20 minutes to 1 hour, depending on the size of the crack, plus drying time

A portland cement and water mixture is fine for foundation and walkway cracks, but use a gravel mix for repairing large cracks on driveways. A gravel mixture is made from 1 part portland cement, 2 parts sand, and 3 parts gravel. When combined, it should be the consistency of a thick paste, like peanut butter.

What You Need

Garden hose with spray nozzle	Cement adhesive
Wire brush	Portland cement and water mixture
Chisel	or gravel mixture
Hammer	Putty knife or trowel
Safety glasses	Plastic drop cloth

How to Get It Done

1. Thoroughly clean the crack with the spray nozzle of your hose. Brush out any remaining debris with a wire brush.
2. Open the crack with a chisel and hammer. This works on the same principle as opening a crack in plaster, which I talked about earlier. This extra depth and width increases the strength of the repair job. Wear safety glasses during this procedure!
3. Brush cement adhesive into the crack.
4. Apply the patch mixture with a putty knife or trowel. Force the mixture into the crack as much as possible. Then smooth it off so it is level with the original concrete.
5. Allow the patch to dry for about 2 hours. Then cover the area with a piece of plastic drop cloth.
6. Keep the area covered for about 5 days. Lift the covering once each day and sprinkle the area with water.

Note: If the patch is on a driveway, don't drive a car over the patch for at least 5 days. This gives the patch time to dry and cure before carrying heavy loads.

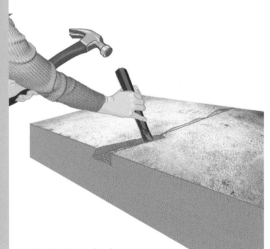

Step 2. Use a chisel and a hammer to open up the crack.

Deck Maintenance

Another important maintenance job is keeping your deck, if you're lucky enough to have one, spick-and-span. It's expensive to replace a deck, but if you take care of yours, it will last longer. After all, decks take a hard beating every year. Snow, rain, hail, sleet—all the elements conspire against a deck, and after a while, its water proofing coating and stain can appear worn or can disappear entirely. Moss buildup and dirt can also ruin a deck's appearance and shorten its life.

Staining your deck does more than just make it look good. It protects the wood from sun and water damage and helps restore natural oils. You don't have to hire an expensive pro to renew your decking. For instance, a neighbor of mine has a gorgeous deck looking out over her backyard. It was looking a bit dull, but I showed her how easy it is to clean and stain it on her own. She immediately had a celebratory barbecue.

SAFETY NOTE

An electric pressure washer can be used for the heavy cleaning process, but keep in mind that it can be hazardous. The force of the water can cause injury to people, animals, or even any loose siding or shingles on your house. If you do rent one, follow the rental company's instructions for use and make sure your work area is completely clear of potential hazards.

All Hands on Deck
Clean and Stain a Deck
Time: 2 days

You need a good weather day for this project. Avoid staining the deck in extreme (hot, cold, or windy) weather. Wear old clothes, be sure to wear safety glasses especially when pressure washing, and wear rubber gloves to prevent your skin from getting stained.

What You Need
Rubber gloves
Safety glasses
Warm water
Bleach
Long-handled bristle scrub brush
Deck cleaner
Small bucket or paint roller tray
Wood stain
Large paintbrush or long-handled roller
Small paintbrush

How to Get It Done

1. Put on rubber gloves and safety glasses. Use warm water, bleach, and a long-handled bristle scrub brush to scrub and clean the mildewed and particularly dirty areas of the deck. Apply the deck cleaner, following the manufacturers instructions, and then let the deck dry completely.
2. Pour the stain into a small bucket or paint roller tray. Using the large paintbrush or long-handled roller, apply a few strokes, working quickly to roll or brush the stain onto the deck. Apply the stain lightly and evenly without overlapping the edges. Use the small paintbrush for hard-to-reach places, like deck railings and corners.
3. Allow the stain to set for at least 24 hours, then sit back and enjoy a cold drink on your newly stained deck.

A Bouquet of Beautiful Ideas

Outdoor maintenance is a necessity, no matter what the size or style of your home. But there are many simple projects you can do to enhance your yard, too. Keeping the lawn mowed and the plants watered is easy enough. Little details, such as a freshly painted door (see "Exterior Doors" on page 114 for great front door tips), a beautiful pathway, a new mailbox, and window boxes will add to the tidy, welcoming look of your front yard. Even hanging lights for a party adds additional personality to your landscape. And if you're fortunate enough to have an outdoor shower, creating a privacy surround for it will help turn your yard into a true sanctuary!

My path needs help!

On the Right Path
Create or Repair a Flagstone Path
Time: A weekend

One of the first things I added to my yard was a random pattern flagstone path. I used large pieces, so I had a strong male friend help me move them in exchange for a barbecue dinner. But smaller pieces make a beautiful path, too, and you may be able to lift them yourself or with the help of a friend. You can also use uniform square stones. Check out what's available at your local nursery or stone yard. And remember, when lifting anything heavy, use your knees, not your back, to do the work!

What You Need
    Able-bodied friend, spouse, or teenager
    Chalk and chalk line or hose
    Shovel
    Sod cutter or edger
    Enough construction-grade sand to cover the area to a depth of 2 to 3 inches
    Wheelbarrow
    Flagstones of various sizes or uniform sizes, depending on the look you want
    Carpenter's level
    Rubber mallet
    50–50 mixture of sand and black topsoil or clay soil
    Utility broom
    Hose with spray nozzle

How to Get It Done
1. If you can, enlist someone else to help with this project. Determine the location of your path, and mark out the length and width with a chalk line. You can also mark it with a hose.
2. Using the shovel, dig out the path to a depth of 3 inches. Be sure to remove any roots and weeds and clear the area so that only soil remains. Tamp down the soil with your feet to compact it as much as possible. You can use a sod cutter or edger to create a line. These tools are easy to use and can be rented for a few dollars a day at a rental center.

This rocky road is really in need of a redo.

3. Add about a 3-inch layer of sand. The depth of the sand should allow the stones to sit flush with the grass. Use one of the stones to check and adjust the depth as you go. Use a carpenter's level to check that the sand path is true.

4. Put each piece of stone in place and set it with a rubber mallet. Push sand under the edges of each stone until it is level. Continue laying stones, matching contours or edges to allow a bit of space (½ inch to 1½ inches, whatever you desire) between each stone. If you're using random-size stones, place large pieces first and then use smaller pieces to fill in the spaces left.

5. After all the stones are set, sweep a 50-50 mixture of sand and black topsoil or clay soil (I used clay soil, and I think it works best) to form the "grout" between the joints. Sweep away the sand and dirt from the top of the stones and wash down with water using the spray nozzle on your hose.

6. After the path is dry, sweep in more sand and dirt mixture to the joints. You may have to continue the sweeping and washing process for a couple of days until the joints are tightly filled.

Step 2. Dig out 3 inches of soil and rubble.

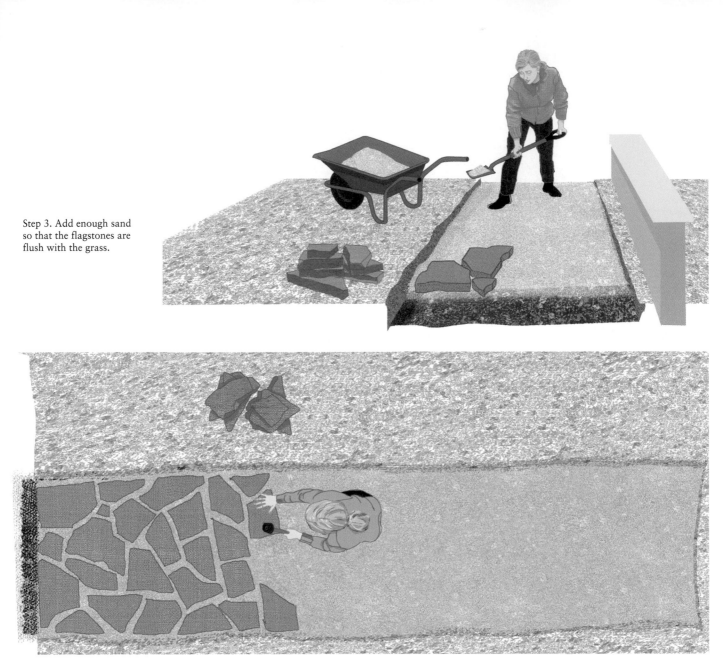

Step 3. Add enough sand so that the flagstones are flush with the grass.

Step 4. Once each stone is in position, set it in place with a rubber mallet.

A flagstone walk is a lovely, permanent landscape feature.

Mail Call
Install a Curbside Mailbox
Time: About 1½ hours

Why not build a pretty path to a brand-new curbside mailbox? A shiny new mailbox adds style and function to your front yard—and makes life a little easier for your mail carrier. Look for an extra-large box and consider painting it in a color to match your house.

If you are installing a mailbox in a new location, call your local utility companies before you begin to dig. They will come out and mark your property so that you know the location of underground cables and pipes. Select the right placement for your mailbox. Make sure you choose a site at least 40 inches away from your driveway to allow for sufficient clearance for vehicles. Your local postmaster can tell you the proper height of the box and the distance it should be from the street. City requirements can vary, so it's worth checking. Generally, the bottom of the mailbox should be between 42 and 48 inches from the ground (not the curb). The front of the mailbox should be about 6 to 8 inches away from the edge of the street.

When using quick-drying cement to backfill a hole in the ground, you do not need to mix the cement with water. It will harden and cure by absorbing the natural moisture from the soil.

What You Need
- Shovel
- Posthole digger
- Work gloves
- Mailbox and post
- Tape measure
- 40-pound bag quick-drying cement
- Old broom handle or dowel
- 4-in-1 level
- Screws (if not included with the mailbox and post)
- Power drill with screwdriver bits or 6-in-1 interchangeable screwdriver
- Paint or stain to match your house
- Paintbrushes

How to Get It Done

1. Using the shovel, cut away a 12-inch square of ground, saving the soil and sod. Dig down at least 6 inches, then use your posthole digger to make the hole about 28 to 30 inches deep. (This is the hard part.) Wear your gloves and flex those muscles! Place the post in the hole and measure with a tape measure from the ground to the top of the post. It should be between 54 and 60 inches high (so that the bottom of the mailbox is between 42 and 48 inches off the ground).

2. With the post in the hole, begin adding the quick-drying cement. Use a hard instrument, such as an old broom handle or dowel, to tamp the cement firmly into the hole. Fill the hole ¼ to ½ full and then check the post on all sides with your level to make sure it is not leaning in any one direction.

3. Finish adding cement to within 4 inches of the top of the hole, tamping the cement down and checking at least once more with the level to make sure the post isn't listing to one direction.

4. Attach the mailbox to the post using screws. Make sure the pole is clean and free of cement residue then paint or stain it to match your house.

5. Replace the soil and sod around the base of the mailbox. You do not have to wait for the cement to set. Cover all of the cement with dirt and sod; do not allow any cement to show.

6. If you wish, paint or stain the mailbox to match your house.

7. Write yourself a letter of recommendation!

Step 2. Check to be sure that the mailbox post is level.

Step 5. Replace the soil around the post.

Flower Power
Build a Window Box Planter
Time: About 2 hours

Window boxes are another great way to add charm and color to the front of your house (although there's nothing stopping you from installing them in the backyard windows). You can change the flowers with the season—annual petunias or impatiens in the spring and summer, mums in the fall. Or you can fill them with dwarf evergreen shrubs for year-round greenery. Plant herbs, and you'll have a window kitchen garden.

Consider painting the boxes to match the color scheme of your house. You can paint the boxes to match your trim or choose an entirely different but coordinating color that blends with both the house and the trim color. Staining the wood gives the boxes a rustic and natural look, especially pretty with shingle-style homes. Crisp, glossy white gives boxes an old-fashioned appeal. Have fun and get your kids involved! Painting is a job many children can help with.

What You Need

2 pieces of 8-foot cedar or redwood 1- by 8-inch board

Power drill

Water-resistant wood glue

2½-inch galvanized screws

Wood buttons (to cover screw holes)

Waterproofing sealer, stain, or paint

Paintbrushes

Silicone caulk

Bedding plants

Stones

Potting soil

How to Get It Done

Step 2. Lay out the pieces and dry-fit them together.

1. Determine the measurements for your window box based on the width of your window. For a 4-foot window, cut two 6- by 48-inch pieces for the front and back of the planter. Cut one 6- by 48-inch piece for the bottom. Cut two pieces from the scrap boards to measure 6 inches wide and 8 inches tall. For the anchor pieces, cut three 6-inch-long pieces.

2. Lay out the pieces and dry-fit them together. Make any necessary adjustments to the pieces.

3. Use a drill to make pilot holes through the faces of the front and back pieces as needed. Drill pilot holes along the bottom face of the bottom piece. For example, a 48-inch window should have four holes, drilled at 12-inch intervals. Glue the pieces together. Place the 1½-inch screws about ½ inch from each end and then roughly every 8 inches to attach the pieces together. Use wood buttons to cover the holes.

4. Drill ⅛-inch holes in the bottom of the planter for drainage.

5. Stain and seal the planter.

6. Attach the three 6-inch pieces to the side of the house, ½ inch below the window frame, with 2½-inch screws. (Do not extend these pieces beyond the sides of the window frame.) These strips will act as spacers between the window box and the wall to allow air to circulate between them.

7. Align the back piece of the window box with the tops of the strips. Drill pilot holes through the back of the window box and the strips.

8. After you've secured your strips to the house, apply a bead of silicone caulk along the top edge of the strip. Attach the window box to the strip by screwing three 2-inch screws per strip on an angle, approximately 1 to 2 inches down from the top of the mounting strip.

9. Put a thin layer of stones on the bottom of the planter before adding potting soil. You'll have improved drainage and less soil loss. Now go ahead and plant your bedding plants.

Step 6. Attach the three 6-inch pieces to the side of the house.

Step 9. Go ahead and plant your flowers!

Lights, Hammer, Action!
Hang Party Lights for an Outdoor Event
Time: About 10 minutes

You don't have to wait for the holidays to enjoy the beauty and whimsy of outdoor lights. These days, string lightbulbs come in a wide variety of sizes, colors, and shapes, and some even come with light covers that are themed for holidays and seasons (think ghosts for Halloween and pineapples and other fruits for summertime cookouts). Hanging string lights is such an easy way to brighten up outdoor spaces. Simply find a starting point close to an outdoor electrical outlet to avoid using long lengths of extension cord. Pick an area to hang them near trees, fences, or your house so that there is something to secure the hook, nail, or staple to.

What You Need
Outdoor string lights
Staple gun or hammer and 2-inch nails
Ladder (if you're hanging the lights up high)

How to Get It Done
1. Hold the string of lights to the fence, tree, or siding of your house, and staple the wires to the surface with a staple gun. Be sure to secure them high enough so guests can walk underneath. If staples do not work, hammer a 2-inch nail in halfway, bend the nail up with the hammer, and run the wires over the top side of the nail.
2. Move farther along approximately 4 to 6 feet, pulling the string of lights to take out the slack and repeat the securing process until complete.
3. Plug in and enjoy!

Backyard Farm
Build a Children's Raised-Bed Vegetable Patch
Time: Less than 2 hours

Zachary loves the way the house glitters when I hang string lights for a party or holiday, including his birthday. And I love to do anything that draws him outdoors to enjoy what nature has to offer. It's not that difficult because Zach, like most children, has a natural affinity for playing outside, digging in dirt, and discovering the amazing world of Mother Nature. I know I did: When I was a kid, I *lived* outside in the summertime. I loved digging for worms and catching frogs—even in the Bronx or in Montauk. You couldn't get me in at the end of the day.

My father was very handy, and one of the things he did when we moved to the suburbs was plant a vegetable patch. It wasn't very elaborate; no one from the local garden club was awarding us blue ribbons. But it was just big enough to provide my mom with tomatoes, zucchini, carrots, and pole beans for spring and summer meals. I remember how amazed I was that a few little seeds, so tiny and seemingly powerless, and a couple of little tomato plants, could grow and give us something to eat at the end. I'd help my dad pick the tomatoes and pull carrots from the ground.

When children see vegetables grow and help care for them, they will want to taste them. Growing vegetables with a child has so many amazing results: They learn about the earth and the cycle of life, they learn the responsibility that comes from nurturing plants, and they explore the world of vegetables and will be so much more willing to try them. Why not build a vegetable bed that you and your children can care for? It's easy and fun and a wonderful way to spend time with your child outdoors during the summer. The 3- by 6-foot size of this garden makes it easy to tend and water.

What You Need
Chalk or a hose
Shovel
One set of four raised bed corners (available at garden centers and garden catalogs) to fit a 10-inch-wide plank
Mallet

Two 10- by 8-foot cedar, redwood, or "plastic lumber" planks cut to
make two 4-foot lengths and two 8-foot lengths
Topsoil amended with organic material such as humus (enough to fill
the box 2 inches from the top)
Rake
Pole
Vegetable seeds such as carrots, peas, and lettuce and assorted
seedlings such as tomatoes and peppers
Watering can

How to Get It Done

1. Mark out a 4- by 8-foot sunny area in your yard with chalk or a hose.
2. Remove the grass and the top 3 inches of soil with a shovel.
3. Drive the corner stakes into each of the corners with a mallet.
4. Using the mallet, drive the planks into each side of the corner spikes so they are all attached.
5. Fill the raised bed with the amended topsoil.
6. Rake the soil smooth but don't pack it down.
7. Create rows along the length of the bed, using a pole to make even indentations.
8. Plant the seeds according to the package directions for your region.
9. In other rows, plant the seedlings according to your climate and region requirements. In general, you should dig a hole twice as wide and deep as the rootball. Tomatoes should be planted deeply, up to the first set of leaves.
10. Water well!

Note: Be sure to consult your local nursery for plant care and pest control.

A simple raised bed filled with easy-to-grow veggies is a great way to teach your kids about nature, nurture, and even cooking (when you prepare and eat the resulting bounty).

Privacy Please
Build an Outdoor Shower Surround
Time: About 2 days

Aside from a fancy built-in swimming pool or bubbling hot tub, the most luxurious (and very practical) element of a backyard is an outdoor shower.

If you live near a lake or the beach or if you have a pool, a shower is a great way to keep feet from tracking sand inside. Plus, taking a shower outside is really fun and refreshing, especially during hot summer months. Even if your house doesn't have an outdoor shower (and I realize most do not), you can buy a portable outdoor shower kit at home centers and large discount retailers—for less than $100. These portable showers easily attach to a standard garden hose. They are usually made out of rugged noncorrosive PVC piping and are completely weatherproof. They come attached to a large oval base that you fill with sand, providing stability. An adjustable showerhead and an on/off valve are also usually included in these inexpensive kits.

If you already have an outdoor shower, or if you are planning on purchasing an inexpensive shower kit, consider building a privacy surround for it like I did. A portable surround (and the portable shower) can be placed close to the water source. The shower and hose can be carried into the privacy area. This shower surround creates a comfortable place to hose off, and it makes for a very pretty feature on your lawn.

A simple hook on a 4×4-inch pole is the perfect place to hang a towel or robe.

What You Need

- Shovel
- Garden hose
- Posthole digger
- Bamboo posts
- 4-in-1 level (optional)
- Bamboo screening or fencing
- 18- or 20-gauge galvanized wire or zinc wire
- Sand
- River rock (enough to form the shower "pan")
- Stepping-stones
- Showerhead and handle kit
- Clumping bamboo plants or tall shrubs (optional)
- Screw-in hook and soap dish

How to Get It Done

1. Use a shovel to remove all grass, weeds, and other growth from the area around your shower.

2. Mark out the area where the shower privacy fence will go. I used a garden hose to mark out the curve for the fence.

3. With a posthole digger, dig holes for the bamboo posts. Each hole should be 2½ feet deep for maximum stability. Posts should be placed every 4 to 5 feet. Place the posts in the holes, and backfill with dirt excavated from the area.

4. I didn't worry about setting the bamboo posts exactly level with once another because it's a natural product and the slight variation in height makes the shower look more outdoorsy, but you can check for level if you like with a 4-in-1 level.

5. Once the posts are installed, wrap them with the bamboo screening. Attach the screening by twisting wire through and around each post.

6. Next, fill in the shower basin (or the areas in front of where you will place your portable shower) with a base of sand, and then top it off with river rock. River rock is expensive, so to save money, buy enough only to create a 4-foot-diameter shower pan. The rest of the shower area can be filled with sand and cement pavers, or stepping-stones can be placed in a path leading to the shower.

7. Finish installing the showerhead and shower handles if you have not done so.

8. Decorate the shower surround with clumping bamboo plants or tall shrubs, and attach a screw-in hook and soap dish if you'd like.

Step 3. Use a posthole digger to make holes for the bamboo poles.

Step 5. Tie bamboo screen to the poles with wire.

My outdoor shower looked pretty
lonely before I erected an enclosure
around it. But now it's perfect!

I replanted clumping bamboo around the screen. Be sure to buy clumping bamboo; bamboo that grows on runners will take over your yard (and your neighbor's yard) in no time.

Epilogue

Congratulations! Now you've learned essential skills that can help improve your home. You did it yourself!

Can you see the connection between those skills and how they can help you accomplish goals you are trying to reach in other areas of your life? When we started out together, I said that making your home beautiful inevitably becomes a direct reflection of the power you have to change your life and make it what you want it to be. Spending the time working for what you really want can be hard—but worth it!

Inspiration is all around you everyday, and it is endless. From the walls to the doors and floors to the natural world and the great outdoors, your environment constantly provokes ideas. My imagination percolates each time I take on a challenge or need to find a solution to a problem at home, in my car, at the office, and in my personal relationships. It takes great desire, persistence, and focus to achieve success in these areas, but the result is what we all strive for: happiness and independence.

Accomplishing each project in this book will help you feel more comfortable holding and using tools. The confidence you get will in turn change your life, and the people around you will sit up and take notice. The home enhancement knowledge you now have will help expand every area of your life, whether you're a working woman or a single mom. Hey, hanging a picture frame is still empowering for me—I want every woman to feel the confidence and sense of accomplishment when she relies on herself to get something done. I truly believe that home improvement = self-improvement. It's a proven formula in my life and now, I'd like to think, in yours.

I hope *Room for Improvement* will be your companion on your own self-improvement journey. Good luck and let me know how you do! Please e-mail me at roomforimprovement@barbarak.com.

Credits and Resources

Thanks to the following photographers, stylists, consultants, contractors, and companies for their assistance in creating the photographs in this book.

George Ross
George Ross Photographs
248 Bellevue Avenue
Upper Montclair, NJ 07043
Phone: 973-744-5171
Fax: 973-783-8760
www.georgerossphotographs.com

Lewis Bloom
Lewis Bloom Photographs
500 Deal Lake Drive, Apt. 3C
Asbury Park, NJ 07712
Phone: 732-774-3334
www.lewisbloomphotographs.com

Michelle Bergeron Designs Ltd.
Michelle Bergeron
Cititaste Interiors
Cititaste Events LLC
40 East 66th Street
New York, NY 10021
Phone: 917-648-8833
www.michellebergeron.com

Loren Simons
Prop artist and sourcing
Tiziana Agnello, assistant prop stylist
lsimons
Phone: 917-715-1876
lsimons@nyc.rr.com

Advanced Electrical Solutions
Paul Sanchez
P.O. Box 787
Southampton, NY 11969
Phone: 631-723-0053
Electrical work

Eleanor Whitmore's Garden Shop
P.O. Box 10
Amagansett, NY 11930
Phone: 631-267-3182
Landscaping work

R. B. Carpet, Inc.
NYC Greenwich Southampton
42 Woodland Avenue
Rockville Center, NY 11570
Phone: 516-852-0149
Carpet installation

ABC Carpet & Home
888 Broadway
New York, NY 10003
Phone: 212-473-3000
www.abchome.com
*Duvet cover/sheets master bedroom
(page 67)*

All-Clad Metalcrafters L.L.C.
424 Morganza Road
Canonsburg, PA 15317
Phone: 800-255-2523
www.allclad.com
Pots and pans (page 198)

American Foliage & Design Group, Inc.
122 West 22nd Street
New York, NY 10011
Phone: 212-741-5555
www.lumenfly.com
Fabric lanterns (page 168)

Archipelago
38 Walker Street
New York, NY 10013
Phone: 212-334-9460
www.archipelagoinc.com
*Bedroom bed linens and pillows;
daybed pillows (page 67)*

Beauvais Concepts for Asha Carpets
969 Third Avenue
New York, NY 10022
Phone: 212-888-3730
*Tibetan silk and wool entrance rug
(page 209)*

Carmen's Custom Sewing
Carmen Escudero
P.O. Box 173
Watermill, NY 11976
Phone: 631-726-0093
*Living room and kitchen window
treatments (page 113)*

Carpet One
Liz Claiborne Flooring Collection
www.carpetone.com
Wool stair runner (page 97)

Demis Gnatiuk
New York City and the Hamptons
Phone: 631-445-6460
demis2u@yahoo.com
*Painting and faux finishing throughout
house*

Golden Oldies Ltd.
132-29 33rd Avenue
Flushing, NY 11354
Phone: 718-445-4400
www.goldenoldiesltd.com
Indian metal mantle (page 187)

Hable Construction
230 Elizabeth Street
New York, NY 10012
Phone: 877-HABLE-04
www.hableconstruction.com
*Geometric accent pillows on living
room daybed (page 168), striped blue
pillow on foyer bench (page 210)*

The Home Depot, Inc.
2455 Paces Ferry Road NW
Atlanta, GA 30339-4024
Phone: 800-553-3199
www.homedepot.com
Bedroom closet fittings (page 118)

InsideOut
11 Railroad Avenue
East Hampton, NY 11937
Phone: 631-329-3600
*Kitchen and foyer ceramic vases and
bowls (pages 198, 209)*

Kohler Co.
444 Highland Drive
Kohler, WI 53044
Phone: 800-456-4537
www.kohler.com
Bathroom fixtures (pages 149, 164)

Lars Bolander N.Y.
72 Gansevoort Street
New York, NY 10014
Phone: 212-924-1000
www.larsbolander.com
*Hand-embroidered coral pillows on
entry bench (page 209)*

Metropolitan Design Group
80 West 40th Street
New York, NY 10018
Phone: 212-944-6110
Paisley pillow in the bedroom (page 67)

Mike Bernstein Paperhanging
New York-Florida
Phone: 888-936-5350
*Grasscloth wallpaper in entry
(page 209)*

Stencil Ease
P.O. Box 1127
Old Saybrook, CT 06475
Phone: 800-334-1776
www.stencilease.com
Stencil on bedroom wall (page 66)

West Elm
Williams-Sonoma, Inc.
3250 Van Ness Avenue
San Francisco, CA 94109
Phone: 866-West-Elm
www.westelm.com
*Platform bed (page 67), end tables
(page 67), bathroom accessories
(page 146), Capiz shell curtain
(page 211)*

Index

Boldface page references indicate photographs and illustrations.
Underscored references indicate boxed text.

Bucket paint pourer, 15–16, **15**
Burn spots on carpet, removing, 101

C

Cabinets
  drawers, freeing stubborn, 175
  handles of, changing, 182–83, **182,**
    183
  painting, 184–85
Cable
  armored, <u>131</u>
  ties, 9, **9**
  wire, <u>131</u>
Can paint pourer, 15–16, **15**
Carpenter's square, 15, **15**
Carpeting
  berber, <u>98</u>
  binding of, <u>98</u>
  broadloom, <u>98</u>
  burn spots on, removing, 101
  density of, <u>98</u>
  hand feel of, <u>98</u>
  ink on, removing, 99
  nylon, 96
  pile of, <u>98</u>
  plush, <u>98</u>
  ply of, <u>98</u>
  pros and cons of, 96
  red wine on, removing, 100
  saxony, <u>98</u>
  sisal, <u>98</u>
  as sound muffler, **96**
  terminology, <u>98</u>
  tiles, 98, <u>98</u>
  tufted, <u>98</u>
  vacuum cleaners and, <u>99</u>
  wax on, removing, 100
  wool, 96, **97**
Casement windows, 104
Caulking gun, 16, **16**

C-clamp, 8, **8**
Ceramic tile, <u>88</u>
Ceramic tile floors
  broken tile, replacing, 94–95
  installing, 88–89
  mosaic sheet tiles and, 90–92, 90, <u>91</u>, 92,
    93
  terminology, <u>88</u>
  thinset mortar and, <u>89</u>
Chair, tightening loose, 176–77, **177**
Chair leg, repairing broken, 178–79,
    179
Chalk line, 15, **15**
Chemical drain openers, <u>161</u>
Chipping paint, fixing, <u>38</u>
Chisels, 10, **10**
Circuit, <u>129</u>, <u>131</u>
Circuit breaker, <u>129</u>, <u>131</u>
Circuit map, 133
Clad wood windows, <u>106</u>
Clamps
  C, 8, **8**
  corner, 8, **8**
  spring, 8, **8**
  web, 8, **8**
Clamshell digger, 20, **20**
Closet auger, 18, **18**
Closets
  bedroom, 202–3, **203, 204**
  for clutter control, 202–3, **203, 204**
  pantry, 202
  sliding doors on, installing, 126–27, **126**
Clutter control
  closets for, 202–3, **203, 204**
  donation of items for, 192
  entryway, 208, **208, 209**, 210, **210**
  home office equipment, <u>206</u>
  lighting accessories, <u>206</u>
  memorabilia, <u>206</u>
  personal sanctuary, creating clutter-free,
    212, **213**, 214–15, **215**
  photographs, <u>206</u>

opportunities for changing and improving, 73

safety issues, 73

variety of, 73

vinyl

    patching, 86–87, **86**, **87**

    pros and cons of, 84

    tile replacement and, 85

wood

    "attic stock" and, 82

    caring for, 74–75

    dent in, repairing, 79

    gaps in, fixing, 81

    gouge in, repairing, 80

    materials for, 74, 75

    painting, 82–83

    scratched, repairing, 77–78, 78

    terminology, 75

Flush valve, 158

Flush valve seat, 158

Folding ladder, 14, **14**

Folding ruler, 14–15, **14**

Furniture, painting, 184–85

Furring strip, 44

Fuse, 131

Fuse map, 133

G

General lighting, 134

Glasses, safety, 6–7, 12

Glass panes

    in door, 117

    double-pane, 104

    replacing broken, 107

    single-pane, 104

    tempered, 104

Glazed tile, 88

Gloss paint finish, 29

Glue, wallpaper, 54

Greenhouse windows, 104

Grille of door, 117

Gripping tools

    adjustable wrench, 9, **9**

    bench vise, 8, **8**

    cable ties, 9, **9**

    C-clamp, 8, **8**

    corner clamp, 8, **8**

    slip joint pliers, 9, **9**

    spring clamp, 8, **8**

    web clamp, 8, **8**

Grounding wire, 131

Grout, 88

Grout float, 14, **14**

Guns

    caulking, 16, **16**

    staple, 12, **12**

H

Hacksaw, 19, **19**

Hammers

    curved claw, 12, **12**

    tack, 12–13, **12**

Hand auger, 18, **18**

Hand feel of carpeting, 98

Hardwood, 75

Hex keys, 10, **10**

Hollow-core doors, 117

Home improvements. *See* Clutter control;
        Fast fixes; *specific areas*; Upgrades,
        everyday

Home office equipment clutter control, 206

Hose, fixing leaky, 222

Hot wire, 131

Humidity, caution about painting in, 34

I

Ink spot on carpet, removing, 99

Inspiration board, 32, **33**

safety issues, <u>147</u>
showers
    drain, clearing, 167
    fixtures, selecting, 163, **164**, **165**
    showerhead, replacing, 166
sinks
    chemical drain openers and, 161
    drain, clearing clogged, 155, <u>161</u>,
      167
    drain stopper, cleaning and adjusting
      pop-up, 154
    drain trap, removing, 156
toilets
    clogged or overflow of, clearing, 160,
      160
    handles, adjusting, 159
    parts of, 157, **157**, 158
    running, repairing, 161
    seat, replacing, 162
    terminology, <u>158</u>
tools, 18, **18**
Plunger, 18, **18**, 160, **160**
Plush carpeting, <u>98</u>
Ply of carpeting, <u>98</u>
Polarized receptacle, <u>131</u>
Popped nails, <u>44</u>, 45, **45**
Porcelain tile, 88
Porcelain tile floors
    broken tile, replacing, 94–95
    installing, 88–89
    mosaic sheet tiles and, 90–92, **90**, <u>91</u>,
      92, **93**
    terminology, <u>88</u>
    thinset mortar and, <u>89</u>
Posthole digger, 20, **20**
Pot rack, hanging, **198**, 199–200, **199**,
    200
Power auger, 20, **20**
Pressure washer, electric, <u>228</u>
Primer paint, 28, 31
Pry bar, 12, **12**
Putty knife, 14, **14**, 46, 47

Q

Quarter-sawn wood, <u>75</u>

R

Raised-bed vegetable patch, building,
    239–40, **241**
Raised paneling, <u>68</u>
Receptacle
    polarized, <u>131</u>
    safety cap, <u>132</u>
    tester, 11, **11**
Reclaimed wood, <u>75</u>
Red wine on carpet, removing, 100
Repeat motif, 54
Rewiring lamp, 142–43, <u>142</u>, **143**
Right hand door, <u>117</u>
Rollers, paint, 16, **16**
Rubbing door, fixing, 121
Rugs. *See* Carpeting
Ruler, folding, 14–15, **14**
Runny paint, <u>38</u>

S

Safety glasses, <u>6–7</u>, <u>12</u>
Safety issues
    chemical drain openers, <u>161</u>
    doors, <u>103</u>
    drilling, <u>6–7</u>
    electric pressure washer, <u>228</u>
    fast fixes, <u>169</u>
    fireplace mantel, building, <u>190</u>
    floors, <u>73</u>
    glasses, <u>6–7</u>, <u>12</u>
    ladders, <u>13</u>, <u>215</u>
    lighting, <u>129</u>, <u>132</u>
    manufacturer's products, <u>25</u>, <u>73</u>, <u>103</u>,
      <u>129</u>, <u>217</u>

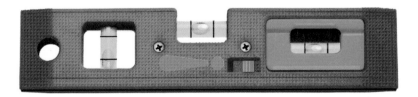